15. FEB 0?.

P|

6/4/13   sou

KT-215-855

‖‖‖‖‖‖‖‖‖‖‖‖‖‖‖‖‖

AUG 2008

Rob**rt Allen** is an experienced lexicographer and writer
on a wide range of language issues. A former Senior Editor of
...rd *English Dictionary*, Chief Editor of *The Concise Oxford*
...*ry* (1990), Associate Editor of *The Oxford Companion to*
...*sh Language* (1992), and Editor of *Pocket Fowler's Modern*
...*Usage* (1999), he has written widely on the use of English
...ern times. He now works as a freelance writer and
...and has written another title for the One Step Ahead
...*pelling*.

22. NOV 07

WITHDRAWN

C151808863

‖‖‖‖‖‖‖‖‖‖‖‖‖‖‖‖‖

One Step Ahead ...

The *One Step Ahead* series is for all those who want and need to communicate more effectively in a range of real-life situations. Each title provides up-to-date practical guidance, tips, and the language tools to enhance your writing and speaking.

Series Editor: John Seely

Titles in the series

Acknowledgements

I have benefited greatly from access to the British National Corpus, a computer database of 100 million words of English collected by a consortium of publishers and academic institutions from a wide range of printed and spoken sources. This invaluable material provided me with an enormous amount of evidence of punctuation practice, which played an important role in the writing of this book.

I should like to thank my colleagues in the One Step Ahead series: in particular the series editor, John Seely, for his advice and encouragement, and Alysoun Owen and Helen Cox at Oxford University Press for their support and help.

Jenny Ollerenshaw and Lucinda Coventry read an earlier version of the text and made some useful suggestions, for which I am grateful. Thanks are also due to Sarah Barrett for the far from easy task of copy-editing.

I cannot close these acknowledgements without thanking the cartoonist, Beatrice Baumgartner-Cohen, for her sensitive and imaginative realization in visual form, in this book and in the companion book on English spelling, of the thoughts that pass through the mind in writing about these aspects of the written language. I hope readers will enjoy them as much as I have.

Robert Allen
Edinburgh
October 2001

Punctuation

Robert Allen

Cartoons by Beatrice Baumgartner-Cohen

KENT ARTS & LIBRARIES	
C151808863	
Cypher	30.09.02
	£6.99

OXFORD
UNIVERSITY PRESS

OXFORD UNIVERSITY PRESS

Great Clarendon Street, Oxford OX2 6DP

Oxford University Press is a department of the University of Oxford.
It furthers the University's objective of excellence in research, scholarship,
and education by publishing worldwide in
Oxford New York
Auckland Bangkok Buenos Aires Cape Town Chennai
Dar es Salaam Delhi Hong Kong Istanbul Karachi Kolkata
Kuala Lumpur Madrid Melbourne Mexico City Mumbai Nairobi
São Paulo Shanghai Singapore Taipei Tokyo Toronto
with an associated company in Berlin

Oxford is a registered trade mark of Oxford University Press
in the UK and in certain other countries

Published in the United States
by Oxford University Press Inc., New York

© Robert Allen 2002

The moral rights of the author have been asserted
Database right Oxford University Press (maker)

First published 2002

All rights reserved. No part of this publication may be reproduced,
stored in a retrieval system, or transmitted, in any form or by any means,
without the prior permission in writing of Oxford University Press,
or as expressly permitted by law, or under terms agreed with the appropriate
reprographics rights organization. Enquiries concerning reproduction
outside the scope of the above should be sent to the Rights Department,
Oxford University Press, at the address above

You must not circulate this book in any other binding or cover
and you must impose this same condition on any acquirer

British Library Cataloguing in Publication Data
Data available

Library of Congress Cataloging in Publication Data
Data available

ISBN 0-19-860439-4

10 9 8 7 6 5 4 3 2 1

Design and typesetting by David Seabourne
Printed in Spain by Bookprint S.L., Barcelona

Contents

Part A
About this book

This book sets out to answer three key questions about punctuation:

Three key questions

- What is it for?

- Why does it seem so complicated?

- How can you improve yours?

If you are reading this book, you will probably realize that punctuation matters and that you can improve yours. This is true for practically everyone. Many people are scared by it because they see it as a sort of code—a myth that this book will seek to dispel. Punctuation is a tool, or rather a set of tools. They are there to help you, and as with actual tools you will need to use some of them more than others.

What it's all for

Chapters 1 and 2 describe what punctuation is for and why it matters.

Helping yourself

Chapter 3 gives you practical advice on how to help yourself to use punctuation correctly and effectively.

Strategies

Chapters 4–7 give you the strategies for organizing your writing by means of punctuation.

Chapter 8 lists some special uses of punctuation: for example, in abbreviations and in writing dates and addresses.

At the end of the book there is a Reference section which gives you basic information organized under headings based on each of the major punctuation marks. This part of the book serves as a checklist, and also describes some of the more common errors in everyday punctuation.

British and American punctuation

This book is mainly about British punctuation. The principles are much the same in American English but there are some differences. For example, quotation marks are used differently.

When there is an important difference between British and American English, this is mentioned.

These differences have become more important because of the influence of American English throughout the world, for example to learners of English and to users of the Internet, where American technology predominates.

In spite of the advantages enjoyed by users of American spelling, in Britain people will expect you to use British spellings and will normally regard American usage as unsuitable or incorrect.

A note on the examples

In this book, nearly all the examples of punctuation are taken from real writing, and even the very short ones are based on actual usage. They are not made up.

This approach, by drawing on real experience in actual usage, illustrates good and bad punctuation much more clearly and effectively than the invented examples you often find in books of this kind.

Seeking and using real examples from real English also formed an important part of the plan in organizing this book. Many of the issues we shall look at are familiar (for example the confusion between semicolons and colons), but hard evidence of what is actually being written can provide many important clues about the day-to-day difficulties people encounter.

1   What is punctuation for?

Getting it in perspective

Some punctuation guides make the mistake (in my opinion) of
starting with a passage of English from which all the punctuation has been removed. The idea is that you can't make head or
tail of it, or at least that you stumble over it and scratch your
head; but in every case that I have seen it's possible to work out
what's going on. In fact it's quite fun. The point is that poor
punctuation makes things difficult for the reader.

Don't be alarmed by
punctuation. It's not
a code, but a way of
making your writing
clearer.

Punctuation is not a kind of code, but is there to make what
you write clear and easy to read. You should only use it as far as
you need it in your writing as part of the process of communi-
cating with your readers. It is useful, and it is important, and
people expect it to be accurate. But we shouldn't make exces-
sive claims for its importance or regard it as a fundamental
part of language in the way that grammar (for example) is.

Punctuation has a single and practical purpose: to make writing clear and easy to understand. Think of your writing as a
set of information rather like a rail timetable or a page on an
Internet website. All the information can be there but if it is
badly laid out it will be confusing and hard to understand.

In writing, the full stops, commas, semicolons, and so on do the same job as the spaces, columns, and special signs on a timetable and the graphics and other ways of organizing the information on a web page.

How can punctuation help your writing?

There are six main ways in which punctuation can make your writing clearer:

A six-point plan for making punctuation work for you

■ Full stops, commas, semicolons, and colons mark out the basic structure of what you are writing.

See Chapters 4 and 5.

■ Dashes and brackets can show groups of words that form a smaller group on their own within a sentence.

See Chapter 5.

■ Question marks, exclamation marks, and quotation marks show that what you are writing is something other than a simple statement by the writer.

See Chapter 4 and (for quotation marks) Chapter 6.

■ The apostrophe and hyphen can link related words and show other special functions.

See Chapter 7.

■ Full stops can show that a group of letters form an abbreviation.

See Chapter 8.

■ An apostrophe can show that letters are missing in a word.

See Chapter 7 beginning on page 44.

We can sum all this up by saying that punctuation operates at two levels:

■ at sentence or phrase level, marking out structure;

See especially Chapter 5.

■ at word level, linking or separating individual words.

See especially Chapter 7.

and punctuation has two main roles:

■ to separate sentences (as full stops do) or separate parts of sentences (as pairs of commas do);

■ to link groups of words into one sentence (as semicolons and colons do).

9

2 Why punctuation matters

How old is it?

How old is punctuation? Who invented it? What on earth for?

If you look at inscriptions in Latin or Greek or other ancient languages on archaeological monuments and remains, there is no punctuation at all, apart from spaces (and sometimes dots) between words and in some cases not even these. So for quite a long time people managed without any form of punctuation. Why then do we get so hung up about it now?

There are several reasons. The ancient languages were heavily inflected, i.e. they had special word endings to show the function of every word in its sentence. And the language you see in inscriptions on ancient monuments was based on often-repeated formulas that would have been familiar to the people reading them. So spaces between words, and occasionally dots to mark the ends of sentences, were all that was needed.

But the ways in which language is used have changed enormously over the centuries. In modern times, many more people can read and write than used to be the case, and reading and writing form an essential part of our everyday lives. Can you think of a day when you did not read or write something?

Punctuation as a substitute for tone of voice

The natural form of communication between human beings is speech. People could speak long before they could write, and language developed as a sequence of sounds that could be heard but not, at that stage, visualized or recorded.

In speech, humans use their voices not just to express sounds but to express them in certain ways and in certain relationships to one another, giving special emphasis to important words, using intonation, and varying the volume (or dynamics) of their utterances. There is all the difference in the world between 'Get away' said softly with a smile and a wink and the same words shouted with a scowl.

In writing we do not use the voice and we cannot use intonation and volume as a means of making our meaning clear. These roles are taken on by punctuation. The following longer extract (from *Tom's Midnight Garden* by Philippa Pearce) shows how the natural pauses and rises and falls of the voice are represented in writing by commas, semicolons, dashes, and other marks:

Tom was silent, turning over in his mind what Hatty had just said. He was beginning to change his mind about climbing the wall, because he saw that there could not be—for him—the danger that there had been for James. He might possibly fall off the wall, but a fall, even from such a height, could neither bruise nor break him.

He said to Hatty, 'I'm going to see if there really is a nest behind the sundial; I'm going to walk along that wall.'

'Oh, Tom!'

The way in which Hatty said, 'Oh, Tom!' made Tom feel warm and kind. He patted her hand. 'Don't worry. It's all right for me.'

He climbed, by means of the laddering branches of the espalier pear, to the top of the wall. In spite of all he had told himself, he felt a pang of horror when he stood upright upon it. The wall top was so narrow—nine inches, in some places weathered away to even less by the crumbling of brickwork; quite bushy plants grew along it, over which Tom would have to step; and on either side of that narrow, hazardous path the wall face went sheer and far: down to the orchard on one side; on the other, down to the garden, where Hatty stood, her pale face upturned to him. Tom knew, however, that he must not look down, if he were to keep his head and walk that wall top. He lifted his eyes and stepped resolutely forward.

Smileys and emoticons

In emails, we can express moods by using 'emoticons' made from punctuation marks. For example, :-) expresses happiness and :-(expresses sadness or disappointment. These are sometimes called 'smileys'.

Early printing

Wherever there is writing, some form of punctuation is not far behind. As far back as the eighth century, during the rule of the emperor Charlemagne, a Northumbrian scholar named Alcuin developed a new system of spelling and punctuation for use in biblical texts and sacred liturgies. The invention of printing in the 15th and 16th centuries meant that written texts would be circulated much more widely than handwritten manuscripts could be, and some regulation of the words on the page was essential. The early printers, for example two Venetians called Aldus Manutius (the second the grandson of the first) and William Caxton in England, played an important part in developing a regular system of punctuation for their printed work.

The superhighway

Most recently, the development of electronic communications, especially faxes, email, and text messaging, has made written communication between people almost as instant as spoken conversation. This form of communication therefore tends to be conversational in style, and punctuation has an important role to play in replacing the intonation we would use in speech.

How does punctuation help you?

2 Why punctuation matters

Punctuation is a tool and is there to help you.

Everyone knows instinctively that punctuation is important, and it is easy to become afraid of it. People see it as some kind of code that only very clever people can master. But that's not true. Punctuation matters because it's a useful tool that is all the more useful if you use it properly. But there's a lot you can learn; and what you can't learn you can master by practice.

It helps you to get your meaning across.

Some people even think that punctuation is more important than spelling, and one can see why. You can usually understand a piece of writing that contains a lot of spelling mistakes, but it's not easy to understand writing that has perfect spelling but is badly punctuated. The way you use the main tools of punctuation, the full stop, the comma, the colon, the semicolon, and so on directly affects the meaning and clarity of what you write.

See Part B, beginning on page 55.

Punctuation has a special place among the key features of language. Unlike grammar and spelling, it is not a part of the structure of language. It is a set of tools that enable you to organize what would otherwise be a continuous string of words. Historically, it is closely related to the structure of written language, and most of the special names (*period, comma, colon, apostrophe*) originally referred to types of sentence and phrase and only later to the special symbols used to mark them. For example, *colon* was a term for a clause, and *comma* was a term for a phrase.

You could say that punctuation is to writing and printing what stitching is to a piece of clothing. Stitches hold a garment together and help to give it its shape, and punctuation, in a sense, holds together the words on a page. It is there to help us.

Are there fixed rules?

There are some rules in punctuation: for example, you always begin a sentence with a capital letter and end it with a full stop. That is an old rule that has not changed. Other rules have changed over many years and continue to change. There are fashions in punctuation, and different types of writing call for different styles of punctuation.

There is a minor character in Dickens's *Nicholas Nickleby* called Mr Curdle, who claims to have proved

> that by altering the received mode of punctuation, any one of Shakespeare's plays could be made quite different, and the sense completely changed.

And in a modern edition of Gibbon's *Decline and Fall of the Roman Empire* (a work first published in the second half of the eighteenth century), the editor tells his readers plainly that

> I have taken the liberty of repunctuating and reparagraphing Gibbon throughout. By today's standards, a reader would have every right to complain that Gibbon used too much punctuation and too few paragraphs.

Punctuation is there to help both writer *and* reader make sense of a text.

This sort of editorial intervention is needed because styles of punctuation have changed over the centuries. Some older writing is smothered in commas and semicolons, and can go on for most of the page without starting a new paragraph. Nowadays we tend to be more sparing in the use of commas and semicolons, and to divide writing into smaller paragraphs. The reason is partly a matter of fashion, but there is a lot of variation in styles, and publishing houses can differ widely in their approach to some issues (notably the comma).

Helping yourself

3

Punctuation is there to help you

The key test of clear effective punctuation is whether you notice it or not. If the writing reads well, you probably won't be aware of all the commas and full stops and semicolons for most of the time.

This is the effect you need to achieve on people who are reading what you write; the less they notice how you have punctuated it the more successful you have been.

Punctuation is there to help you, and should not be seen as a kind of ordeal like a compulsory question in an exam.

Use the punctuation marks that you are most comfortable with. For most of the time these will be full stops and commas, which you really can't avoid.

Try to get the balance right: too many punctuation marks are confusing, like too many signs on a motorway, while too few can make your writing hard to follow.

Tips
- Use punctuation to make your writing clearer.
- Use a style that suits you and your readers.
- Note the ways other people use punctuation.
- Use the tip boxes in this book to help you.

When you have no choice

Sometimes the choice of punctuation marks is straightforward, and there is only one that is right. For example, a sentence that is a statement always ends in a full stop, a question ends in a question mark, and direct speech always has quotation marks round it.

Making choices

Tips
- Don't agonize over choices: often more than one possibility will do.
- Use the tips to help you.

Most people need guidance when there is a choice of punctuation, for example between commas and semicolons. The choices are not always clear-cut, and if you can't decide it's often a sign that either choice will work. Remember that punctuation is a practical matter. In the end, what matters is that your writing is clear to read.

For example, when I was writing the first sentence in the previous section, first of all I wrote it like this:

> Sometimes the choice of punctuation marks is straightforward: there is only one that is right.

Then I read it again and thought that the colon was too strong, and produced a kind of anticlimax, so I rewrote it like this:

> Sometimes the choice of punctuation marks is straightforward, and there is only one that is right.

If I had gone on to give a list of various punctuation marks in the same sentence, then a colon might have been justified. But I didn't, and the sentence ended fairly simply.

If you have problems making choices, whether between commas, semicolons, and colons, or between commas, dashes, and brackets, there are several things you can do to help yourself:

You try
A checklist for your writing

- Do your sentences begin with capital letters and end in full stops?
- Are your sentences the right length?
- Do you have too many commas?
- Could you use more semicolons and colons?
- Are your quotation marks and apostrophes in the right positions?

■ Look at the guidance given in Chapters 1–3 of this book.

■ Notice punctuation when you are reading, and choose different types of reading: novels, non-fiction, newspapers, informal writing, and so on. See how the punctuation differs in a very formal piece of writing, such as a report or textbook, from that in much more informal writing, such as a letter from a friend. The chances are that the more formal writing will contain more semicolons and colons, while the informal writing will have a lot more commas.

Choose different types of reading

■ Make a note of bad punctuation as well as good, for example in personal and business letters you receive. See how it affects your understanding of what is written. When you come across something that is unclear in what you are reading, see if changing the punctuation makes it clearer.

■ Read through your own writing and see if you can make changes that would bring out the meaning more effectively.

Different styles

The punctuation used in this book falls somewhere between the formal and informal styles; for example, you will probably find more semicolons than you are used to using (there is one in this sentence).

Noticing these differences will help you to decide:

■ which approach suits you and your readers best;

■ how punctuation helps to make writing clear.

You try
Look at different types of printing and see how the punctuation differs.

Remember that the approach you find most suited to you is likely to be the one that makes your writing clearest for your readers. The amount and type of punctuation you need will change with the type of writing you are doing.

You are likely to need less guidance on punctuating informal English because it doesn't matter so much, as long as you are understood. Some punctuation rules, for example on showing direct speech, are mostly confined to special areas of writing such as creative writing.

Tip
You need to be especially careful when writing to impress people, e.g. in job applications, when you will be judged on your presentation.

You are most likely to need guidance when you are writing material, such as job applications, business letters, and reports, that is regarded as 'formal' and should follow set conventions and avoid the looser informalities of language that are associated with casual speech and conversation. Most of the guidance in this book has this priority in mind.

Things you can learn

Punctuation follows rules that you can learn. For example:

See pages 21, 26, and 57.

■ full stops at the end of sentences;

See pages 27 and 59.

■ commas: the difference between single commas and commas used in pairs;

See pages 37 and 66.

■ colons used in lists;

See pages 40 and 75.

■ quotation marks in direct speech;

See pages 45 and 85.

■ hyphens, e.g. the difference between *twenty-odd people* and *twenty odd people*;

See pages 46 and 78.

■ apostrophes, e.g. the difference between *the boy's work* and *the boys' work.*

Building paragraphs and sentences

4

The main units of writing

There is more to punctuation than a lot of commas, full stops, and other signs that mark your writing. The way you arrange your writing in sentences, paragraphs, and larger sections is also important to getting your message across clearly. This book will help you to organize your writing at various levels: from word to word, from sentence to sentence, and from page to page.

The largest text unit in an ordinary piece of writing, such as a letter or short report, is the paragraph. In longer and more formal writing, such as books and long reports, there are larger divisions into chapters and sections.

Each paragraph should contain a complete concept or train of thought, or—if you are writing a story or narrative—a single event. When you move on to a new thought or idea, you should start a new paragraph. Remember that some paragraphs can be quite short. Getting the balance right is important, because too many paragraphs make your writing disjointed and disturb the flow of the information you are giving, whereas too few paragraphs make your writing hard to read and can make your arguments too dense.

Hierarchy of main units in writing

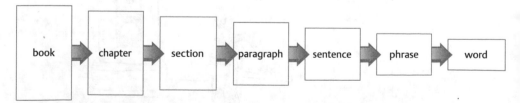

book → chapter → section → paragraph → sentence → phrase → word

Organizing words into sentences

What is a sentence?

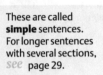

Unlike paragraphs, which are a way of organizing writing into units of thought, sentences are units of language in speaking as well as writing. People often agonize over exactly what is and is not a real sentence, and some grammars spend several pages trying to define the term, but the important point is what a sentence does.

A sentence can do several things:

■ It can make a statement

It was half past four in the afternoon.

These are called
simple sentences.
For longer sentences
with several sections,
see page 29.

■ It can ask a question

Will you be all right?

■ It can express a command or order

Come and sit here.

■ It can express an exclamation

That hurt!

20

Statements

A sentence usually contains a verb that expresses the action or state that the sentence is all about, but it doesn't have to contain a verb, especially in less formal writing or for special effect. Here is the beginning of a modern novel (*The Good Terrorist*, by Doris Lessing). The first sentence contains a verb (*was*) but the next two sentences do not; in a sense they 'borrow' the verb from the first sentence without stating it:

> The house was set back from the noisy main road in what seemed to be a rubbish tip. A large house. Solid.

Some questions and exclamations can be single words such as *Really?* or *Nonsense!*

In more formal writing, such as reports and business letters, your sentences would normally be complete and contain a verb. This is because of the type of information or statement you are concerned with: much less like ordinary conversation (which is full of partial and incomplete sentences) and more like a series of formal arguments.

What is special about a sentence, whether or not it contains a verb, is that it begins with a capital letter and ends with a full stop, and expresses a complete thought. These features are always essential:

> No poet is ever completely lost. He has the secret of his childhood safe with him, like some secret cave in which he can kneel. And, when we read his poetry, we can join him there.

Questions

If a sentence asks a question, you put a question mark at the end instead of a full stop:

> Where shall I put the chair?
> Do you remember her?
> Will you help me with this?

A sentence usually contains a verb like *is*, *was*, *goes*, or *took*. But you can have sentences without verbs.

You try
Notice all the different types and lengths of sentences in your reading.

You will find more on question marks in the Reference section beginning on page 55.

But questions that are reported in so-called 'indirect' speech, i.e. by someone referring to what the original speaker said, after a verb like *say*, *ask*, and *enquire* (often called indirect questions), should not have a question mark:

> Where shall I put the chair?

but

> I asked her where I should put the chair.

You can find more about this type of sentence in the section on indirect speech on page 42.

A question can consist of a short phrase or even a single word, especially in written versions of conversations:

> 'Tomorrow?'

Some sentences that are put in the form of questions are in fact instructions, and have a corresponding intonation in speech. In these cases it is usual to omit the question mark in writing or print, for example in notices and handouts:

> Would those wishing to attend the talk on Georgia on Tuesday leave their names with one of the staff before they leave.

Watch out!
Not all questions end in a question mark.

On the other hand, some sentences that are put in the form of statements are really invitations that can be regarded as questions: for example those beginning with an introductory phrase such as *I wonder if/whether …* . This kind of sentence is essentially conversational, and would normally occur in writing only in personal letters or notes or similar casual contexts. In these cases a question mark is optional:

> I wonder if you would like to meet them tomorrow.

> I wonder if you would like to meet them tomorrow?

Beware!
Question marks can come at the end of sentences that don't look like questions.

If the invitation is put in a form that is more like a statement in indirect speech, you should omit the question mark:

> I was wondering if you would like to meet them tomorrow.

Choice depends a lot on the context. At the end of a longer sentence that begins as a statement, for example, it is more natural to regard the whole thing as a statement and omit the question mark:

> Tim and Mary are visiting next week and I wondered if you would like to meet them.

Exclamations

An exclamation can be an order, a cry of surprise, an expression of a feeling such as enthusiasm or regret, or a wish; in fact, any group of words that is addressed strongly and directly to the reader. Exclamations, by their nature, often lack a verb.

In all these cases, you put an exclamation mark at the end:

You will find more on **exclamation marks** in the Reference section beginning on page 73.

> What nonsense, letting politics upset a personal relationship!
> As if she could forget!
> The music's too loud! Please turn it off!
> Aren't they beautiful!
> If only he had said something!

An exclamation, like a question, can consist of a short phrase or single word:

> Good!

> Quiet!

It's quite common in informal writing to use several exclamation marks together for special effect, e.g. *Go away!!* or *They've got ten children!!!*

But in more formal writing you should stick to single exclamation marks.

How long should sentences be?

This is a question that people often ask about sentences and writing style, especially in relation to compound and complex sentences which by their nature tend to be longer than simple ones. The occasional shorter- or longer-than-average sentence is harmless and often effective. What matters is the overall effect of a sequence of sentences. Generally speaking, sentences should not be so short that what you write becomes jerky and difficult to read, nor so long that the reader will find it hard to keep track of what you are saying.

Do!

think about the most appropriate style of writing for your reader.

It also depends quite a lot on the type of writing you are doing. In formal writing, such as reports and business letters, sentences need to be more carefully constructed because they are usually carrying an argument or important point. On the whole they are longer in this kind of writing, whereas in informal writing—for example in personal letters—you would normally expect to write shorter sentences because what you are saying is likely to be easier and more entertaining to read, more like conversation, and there is less at stake in the communication with your reader.

Have you noticed the length of my last sentence? When I read it over again I considered doing two things:

■ dividing it into two sentences at the word *because* (although I would have had to reword that part);

■ making a new paragraph at the start of that sentence.

But I decided that the two parts of the second sentence are too closely connected to split them, and also that the two sentences belong together, although this results in a paragraph that is rather longer than average.

expect to write shorter sentences because you are saying is likely to be easier and more

In the next chapter we will see how three key punctuation marks—the comma, semicolon, and colon—can help to organize sentences and make them flow better.

5 Punctuating sentences

Punctuation works
at **macro** and **micro**
levels.

For **questions**, *see*
page 21.

For **exclamations**,
see page 23.

In this chapter we will see how you can use punctuation to control the structure and shape of whole sentences and make them clear to the reader. We can call this the 'macro-level' of punctuation, rather like a macro-climate relating to large geographical areas. In a later chapter we will see how punctuation operates at a 'micro-level' to control, link, and separate individual words and phrases within sentences.

Using punctuation to organize sentences

How long a sentence can be without becoming awkward to read depends a great deal on how you use the punctuation marks that can help you to organize it.

The punctuation marks that you need to use most of the time are the **full stop (.)**, **comma (,)**, **semicolon (;)**, and **colon (:)**.

You should end every sentence with a **full stop**. If it is a question, you should end it with a **question mark (?)**, and if it is an exclamation, you should end it with an **exclamation mark (!)**.

You can use **commas** in two main ways:

- pairs of commas to separate optional elements or 'asides' from the main structure in any type of sentence

  This would, at a stroke, reduce the rise in prices.

- single commas to organize the parts of longer sentences

  People do what you pay them to do, not what you ask them to do.

You use **semicolons** to link two main clauses to form one sentence

> When a man wants to murder a tiger he calls it sport; when a tiger wants to murder him he calls it ferocity.

You use **colons** to link parts of a sentence when the second part leads on from the first

> His words rang in her head: everything's fine, everything's fine.

When to use commas

Pairs of commas

We will look first at commas used in pairs, because they can occur in simple sentences as well as compound and complex ones.

You use a pair of commas to mark off words that make up a separate group within a sentence and form a kind of aside, rather than being an essential part of the sentence.

This is very common with qualifying words such as *however, of course,* and *as far as you are concerned*:

> The universe that we know, of course, is a tiny fragment of the actual universe.

> Serious pollution, however, is a relatively rare event.

There are two very important rules to remember with pairs of commas:

■ to put in the second comma. If you leave it out it makes the sentence confusing to read and can affect the meaning:

> ✔ The mistake, which they admitted, has proved costly.

> ✗ The mistake, which they admitted has proved costly.

Many people are uncertain about it whether to use a comma or a semicolon or a colon. The rest of this chapter will help you to understand their roles and which you choose in particular types of sentence.

Use commas in pairs to mark off extra words and asides.

For more on
brackets,
see page 38.

The second sentence is incomplete without the second comma, but as far as it goes it suggests that 'they' admitted that the mistake had proved costly rather than that they had made the mistake in the first place.

If you remind yourself that pairs of commas used in this way do the same job as brackets, it will be more obvious that you need both commas, just as you need both brackets.

■ to put the commas in the right place, especially in sentences where there is another comma, for example after a linking word such as *and* or *but*. You can test this by seeing how the sentence looks without the part that is separated by the commas:

> The Bank said it understands their problem, but unless payment is received by the end of the month, it might be forced to repossess the property.

A comma before *but* is quite legitimate, but the comma after *month* calls for a first comma before *unless*, because the part to be separated off is 'unless payment is received by the end of the month'. If you leave this part out, the sentence makes no sense:

> ✗ The Bank said it understands their problem it might be forced to repossess the property.

The correct punctuation in this case is:

> The Bank said it understands their problem but, unless payment is received by the end of the month, it might be forced to repossess the property.

Then the sentence still makes sense when the separated part is left out:

> ✔ The Bank said it understands their problem but it might be forced to repossess the property.

Single commas in longer sentences

As a general guide, remember that commas are used to mark points in the sentence where there is a break in the flow of meaning. This is usually reflected in the grammar of the sentence, and usually also in the way you would speak it. So it is often a good idea, when you are writing, to say the sentence to yourself, or even out loud. This will give you a good idea of where the commas should go. It is important to recognize when commas are necessary, usually to avoid misunderstanding or to support the grammar of the sentence, and when they are optional, producing a different effect depending on whether you put them in or not.

Tip

There are three main kinds of sentence: simple, compound, and complex. These three types have different patterns of grammar.

Simple sentences

A simple sentence has one main verb and subject (together called a clause):

In the examples, the **subject** is in bold type, and the <u>verb</u> is underlined.

> **Words** <u>are</u> our servants.

Compound sentences

Compound sentences are those that have two parts joined by a linking word such as *and* or *but*. You often need a comma in sentences of this type, but not always. The main test is whether there is a break in the flow of the sentence that would be expressed by an actual pause in speech.

You try
Try reading the sentence aloud and notice whether you make a pause: if so, you need a comma

If the sentence is continuous in sense and you would not normally make a pause after the first part, you probably don't need a comma:

> **She** <u>pushed</u> the branches through and then <u>squeezed</u> through the stile herself.

> Not long after **they** <u>came</u> for her and <u>killed</u> her too.

(This is more likely to happen when the linking word is *and*.)

If there is a slight break between the two parts of the sentence, this is a sign that you need a comma:

Tip
You need a joining word (such as *and* or *but*) in compound sentences: *see* page 38 for what to do when there is no joining word.

> **There** <u>are</u> old pilots and foolish pilots, but no old foolish pilots.
>
> **W e** <u>are</u> not all perfect, but **w e** <u>can</u> do something perfect.

(This is more likely to happen when the linking word is *but*, especially when there is no verb in the part after *but*.)

The comma is especially important when the subject of the sentence changes or is repeated:

> **The end of term** <u>came</u>, and **David** <u>passed</u> his examinations.
>
> **The interviewer** <u>hesitated</u>, and when **he** <u>asked</u> the next question he sounded faintly embarrassed.

Complex sentences

Complex sentences are those that have a subordinate clause, i.e. one that cannot stand on its own and is joined to a main clause by a word or phrase such as *if*, *because*, *although*, *as soon as*, or *so that*.

You usually need a comma when the subordinate clause comes at the beginning of the sentence:

In the examples, the **subject** is in bold type, and the <u>verb</u> is underlined.

> As soon as **the guests** <u>had gone</u>, **she** <u>rushed</u> to the telephone.
>
> If **I** <u>ask</u> an engineer how a steam engine works, **I** <u>have</u> a pretty fair idea of the general kind of answer that would satisfy me.

But here too you can leave the comma out when the rhythm of the sentence is continuous and the subject of the sentence remains the same (*he* in the example below):

> As **he** <u>lifted</u> the receiver **he** <u>saw</u> Hilary was standing at the door.

A comma after *receiver* would be quite correct and would put a pause in the sentence at that point. That is why it is important to think about how you want the sentence to sound to the person reading it.

Some sentences need several commas because they have several of the features we have mentioned:

> Beyond, in the distance, a great ridge rose high, running from one side of the window to the other.

Without the use of commas the following sentence would be difficult to follow:

> She had never been able to believe, in some corner of her, that anybody, particularly not a member of the working class, could obey an order to destroy a house.

You need a comma before a subordinate clause that comes at the end of a sentence when there is a definite break in the flow of the sentence:

> It's better to try to take more of an interest and make interesting videos, because if you're a creative person I think you can make creative videos.

> He reached over and pulled Shelley towards him, so that he could put his arm round her waist.

But if the sense is continuous and you would not normally pause in speech, you can omit the comma;

> A hospital cleaner in Barnsley works part-time because she's got two small children.

Tip
You usually need a comma when a clause beginning with *so* (or *so that*) and giving a result or consequence comes at the end of a sentence:

You <u>can</u> deal with much of the coursework during the day, so **your evenings** <u>are</u> free.

Reminder
A **subordinate clause** is one that cannot stand on its own in a sentence, e.g. one beginning with *if* or *because*

Tip
When the main clause has *not* or another negative word in it, a comma is often needed to make the meaning clear:

We will not necessarily be able to prevent such cases from happening again, because human beings are full of frailties.

Reminder
A **subordinate clause** is one that cannot stand on its own in a sentence.

Note that a subordinate clause can be introduced by a verb ending in *-ing* or *-ed* (or *-t* or *-en* in some verbs: these are all called participles). In these cases the same rule about including a comma applies:

> She lay back in the bed, watching the play of moonlight upon the window and listening to the water below.

> The waters ran on, tinkling like a musical box.

> Determined to prove her brother's innocence, she studied to be a lawyer in the evenings and worked as a waitress by day.

Tip
If the verb refers not to the subject of the sentence (e.g. *she* in the last example) but to something else, or to nothing specific in the sentence (as with *given* in the following example), the comma is much more important:

Given that 27 million people recently watched the BBC1 television tribute to Queen Elizabeth, the British fascination with royal-watching seems undiminished.

Relative clauses

See the glossary on page 98 for more help with these terms.

There is a special type of subordinate clause called a relative clause. Relative clauses are introduced by *who*, *which*, or *that*.

There are two types of relative clause, depending on the job it has to do:

■ **defining** or **restricting** clauses;

■ **non-defining** or **non-restricting** clauses.

A **defining** clause identifies the word or phrase it relates to and is an essential part of the sentence. In this type, you can use *that* instead of *which* or *who*, and there is no comma before *which/who/that*:

No comma is needed before a 'defining' clause.

> Have you seen the house which/that looks like a boat?

> What have they done with the money which/that I gave them?

Tip

In the second example, you can also omit that altogether and say:

What have they done with the money I gave them?

If you can do this without wrecking the sentence, you know that you are dealing with a defining type of relative clause and that there shouldn't be a comma before it.

The words *that looks like a boat* and *that I gave them* are needed to convey the meaning because they identify the particular thing (the house and the money) you are talking about.

The other type of relative clause is the **non-defining** type. In this type, the clause is introduced by *which* or *who* and adds additional information that is not an essential part of the structure of the sentence.

In this type of relative clause, you need a pair of commas:

> The money, which totals several millions, comes from anonymous donors.

You need commas with a 'non-defining' clause because the clause has the role of an aside (*see* page 27).

It makes perfect sense to leave out the words between the commas and just say:

> The money comes from anonymous donors.

i.e. the *which*-clause adds purely optional information. This type of clause is called 'non-restricting' because it does not 'restrict' or identify the thing being talked about in any way; it just tells you more about it by the way. (Note that you cannot use *that* in this type of clause.)

Note that there is another way of adding the additional information without using *which*, and that is by using a verb ending in *-ing* in a so-called 'non-finite' relative clause:

> The money, totalling several millions, comes from anonymous donors.

Commas are needed in this type of construction too, because the *-ing* clause is functioning as an aside and not as part of the main structure of the sentence.

Beware!
An *-ing* clause can be restricting too, just like a *that*-clause, and just as in a restricting *that*-clause there is no comma:

The man cleaning the windows looked up at that moment.

(The words 'cleaning the windows' are equivalent to 'who/ that was cleaning the windows' and identify the particular man being spoken about.)

Relative clauses with *which* and *who* need special care, as they (unlike ones with *that*) are capable of being defining or non-defining in type. For example:

Watch out!
Take special care
with *who* and *which*
clauses.

> The children, who are sitting examinations, will not be travelling at their normal time.

> The children who are sitting examinations will not be travelling at their normal time.

The meaning is different in these two sentences. In the first sentence, the commas make the words 'who are sitting examinations' into an aside that does not form the main part of the sentence. The essential meaning is therefore that 'the children (i.e. all the children being talked about) will not be travelling at their normal time'.

Without the commas, as in the second version of the sentence, the words 'who are sitting their examinations' become a restrictive or identifying clause, and the meaning is that these particular children, rather than all of them, will not be travelling at their normal time.

You could also use a non-finite *-ing* clause of the kind we saw above, and put:

Watch out!
In this kind of
sentence, make sure
your commas match
your meaning!

> The children sitting examinations will not be travelling at their normal time.

When to use semicolons

Reminder
semicolon is ;
colon is :

Semicolons are used to divide sentences into longer parts, and have the same structural role as linking words such as *and* or *but* have in compound sentences. Each part is like a smaller sentence in itself, but there is a close connection between the parts that might be lost if you use two separate sentences:

> These few hundred yards are my village; here I am known and recognized and greeted and safe.

You could write this as two separate sentences, but the idea contained in them would come across as two distinct thoughts rather than one thought expressed in two ways:

> These few hundred yards are my village. Here I am known and recognized and greeted and safe.

At the beginning of the 21st century, semicolons are very unfashionable. People tend to avoid them in ordinary writing, and it is the punctuation mark you are least likely to come across if you riffle through a modern novel (some writers for children avoid them on principle as 'too difficult'). This is a pity because, if well used, semicolons can play an important role in organizing sentences and making the meaning clearer and more effective.

People are wary of semicolons because they are not sure about when to use them instead of commas or colons; so they tend to use commas all the time. Note that I have just used a semicolon in the sentence before this one; and I am using one again in this sentence. You can see, I hope, how effective they can be in joining two connected statements that are better expressed as one sentence than as two but need a stronger link than the comma provides.

Semicolon checklist

Use a semicolon to

- join two sentences as one;
- make a stronger division than a comma;
- make a strong division in a sentence that already has commas.

semicolon = balance!

Note that sentences don't have to be very long to need semicolons:

> This is Wednesday; we meet on Friday.
>
> The rich don't have children; they have heirs.

In the last sentence, you could use a comma, but the effect created by the slight pause between the two statements would be lost:

> The rich don't have children, they have heirs.

It is very useful to have a semicolon up your sleeve when you want to make a stronger division in a sentence that already has a lot of commas in it (both this extract and the one below are from *River Boy* by Tim Bowler):

> She looked up at him, expecting him to speak, but he didn't; he just held her, his eyes staring over her head; then—just as suddenly—he let her go.

Here is a longer example:

> She saw pictures of him playing with her in the garden when she was very small, letting her climb all over him, pretending she was too strong for him; pictures of him taking her to hospital the time she fell from the swing and hurt her leg; pictures of him teaching her to ride a bike, holding on to the saddle to steady her and calling out encouragement when he realized she was afraid.

When to use colons

If people are confused about when to use a semicolon instead of a comma, they can be even more confused about the choice between semicolon and colon. Their roles overlap, and so there will often be cases where you could use either; but the effect will be different.

The main difference is this: a semicolon is meant to produce a balance between the two parts of the sentence, whereas a colon produces an effect whereby the meaning in the second part leads on from the first part. There are several ways in which this can happen:

- The first part can be a general statement and the second part an elaboration or explanation of it:

    I have three children: two are grown up but the youngest still lives at home with me.

    He was being made to feel more part of the family: the children kissed him goodnight, like a third parent.

- The second part can be a list of something introduced or mentioned more generally in the first part:

    There are two modes of transport in Los Angeles: car and ambulance.

- The first part can introduce something quoted in the second part:

    This meeting is the result of a small ad which he had placed in the New Statesman. It said: 'Polish gentleman, 50s, political refugee, seeks intellectual woman for marriage.'

    His words rang in her head: everything's fine, everything's fine.

- The two parts can describe a cause and its effect, or a premise and its conclusions:

    You can have your cake and eat it: the only trouble is you get fat.

Colon checklist

Use a colon to

- join two sentences with one leading on to the other;
- introduce a list;
- introduce speech or a quotation.

colon = explanation!

Semicolons and colons linking statements

It's very important to remember that you use a semicolon or colon and not a comma to link two clauses, i.e. two separate statements each having its own grammatical subject (*the car* and *this* in the example below) and not linked by a joining word (conjunction) such as *and* or *but*:

✗ It's a pity **the car** is left-hand drive, **this** is a bit inhibiting.

✔ It's a pity **the car** is left-hand drive; **this** is a bit inhibiting.

An alternative that is often better is to put in a joining word such as *and*, *but*, or *because*:

✔ It's a pity the car is left-hand drive, **because** this is a bit inhibiting.

But when there are more than two statements you can often treat them like a list and use commas:

✔ The French want to attack, the Americans want to bomb, and the British want to have another meeting.

Tip
You can use a comma to join two statements when the first is negative (i.e. it contains a word such as *not* or *never*) and the second is given as a positive alternative to it:

⌁ *I don't hate men, I just wish they'd try harder.*

Brackets and dashes as an alternative to pairs of commas

You can use round brackets (technically called *parentheses*) or a pair of dashes instead of commas to mark off words that do not belong to the main part of the sentence:

The money (which totals several millions) comes from anonymous donors.

Left to itself—and that is what it is when it dies—the body tends to revert to a state of equilibrium with its environment.

Reminder
You will find information on pairs of commas used in this way on page 27.

The effect of using brackets, and especially dashes, is to produce a more informal and relaxed style in the manner of conversation. For this reason they are often preferable in informal writing, such as personal letters.

Brackets are a useful option when the words you want to separate off do not fit the grammar of the sentence as a whole, e.g. they form a complete sentence in themselves:

His subsequent conversion to Christianity (he was born into the Jewish faith) again alienated some of his audience.

and when you want to add words to explain or elaborate on something you have already mentioned:

The only piece of furniture I have so far acquired is a very tiny desk on which I have laid out my papers (this journal, my Hindi grammar and vocabulary, Olivia's letters).

Tip
Brackets and dashes are often interchangeable, but dashes have a more conversational effect.

Tip
There is another kind of bracket, a square bracket, that you can use when you want to add a comment of your own to explain something that might otherwise be unclear in what you are writing:

She stood listening to the steady buzz-buzz [of the phone], imagining the kitchen where it was ringing.

6 Punctuating speech and quotations

Because of their appearance, quotation marks are also called *inverted commas*, but since they don't behave at all like commas this is a less helpful name.

You always use quotation marks in pairs, like brackets. It's important to put quotation marks in the right places in relation to other punctuation.

AmE

Quotation marks

In some kinds of writing you need to quote other people's words, such as conversations, extracts from other writing, or well-known sayings and quotations. In these cases you need to use quotation marks.

Quotation marks tell the reader that the words between them are what someone else has said or written, and so you only use them when you are giving the exact words in their original form.

Quotation marks can be either single (' ') or double (" "). In printing style, it is more usual to use single quotation marks in British practice and double quotation marks in American practice, although there is some variation. Double quotation marks tend to be more common in informal writing on both sides of the Atlantic.

Quoted words can be either another person's words (this is called direct speech) or phrases within sentences. The punctuation rules, especially in relation to other punctuation in the sentence, are different in these two types of quotation.

> *Tip*
> Double quotation marks have the advantage of making things clearer when there are apostrophes in the sentence, which can be confused with closing quotation marks:
>
> *"You'll need to give me two weeks' notice," she told him sternly.*

Direct speech

Direct speech is the exact quotation of another person's words, and in this case the quotation marks go outside other punctuation:

'I hope he's not really hurt,' she said.

'How long will it take us to get there?' he asked.

The usual punctuation mark at the end of the quoted words before mention of the speaker (after *hurt* in the first example above) is a comma. But if the speech is a question or exclamation, a question mark or exclamation mark is used instead, as in the second example.

When the speech is interrupted by mention of the speaker, it can be resumed either as a new sentence (as in the first example below) or, when the sense is continuous, after a comma (as in the second example):

'So that's what real life is like,' Jinny said. 'No money and a mountain of runner beans.'

'Copperfield,' said Mr Micawber, 'accidents will occur in the best-regulated families.'

When the quotation is a short phrase or group of words contained within the structure of the main sentence, the quotation marks go inside other punctuation:

Only in Britain could it be thought a defect to be 'too clever by half'.

All he said was 'how uncomfortable', and quickly lowered his eyes as if afraid of embarrassing me.

If you put one quotation inside another, the inside one has double quotation marks if the main ones are single:

'What do you mean, "news"?' she asked.

Tip
Notice the position of a question mark or exclamation mark when the direct speech comes at the end of the sentence:

Charles said: 'Must you go in?'

- The question mark belongs to the direct speech.
- You don't add a full stop at the end.

Did Charles say 'Must you go in?'?

- There are two questions here.

AmE

In American English double quotation marks are used as the main ones and they always go outside other punctuation:

Only in Britain could it be thought a defect to be "too clever by half."

The choice between single and double quotation marks is the other way round:

"What do you mean, 'news'?" she asked.

41

You will find more examples of all these rules in the Reference section on page 75.

The question mark belongs to the question beginning with 'what' and so it comes at the end of that question before the single closing quotation mark.

Indirect speech

There is another way of setting down other people's words, and this is called indirect speech. In indirect speech, the person speaking or writing reports what another person said, not quoting the actual words but putting them into the context of their own sentence, often with a linking word such as *that*, *if*, or *whether*. In the examples below, the sentence is given first in the form of direct (quoted) speech and then in the form of indirect (reported) speech, so that you can see the difference clearly:

> **direct:** 'I hope he's not really hurt,' she said.

> **indirect:** She said (that) she hoped (that) he wasn't really hurt.

The word *that* after *said* in the second version is optional, and is usually omitted in conversational English (as it is after *hoped* as well).

> **direct:** 'How long will it take us to get there?' he asked.

> **indirect:** He asked how long it would take to get there.

Remember that you do not use quotation marks in indirect speech, only in direct speech:

> ✗ She said 'she hoped he wasn't really hurt.'

> ✗ He asked 'how long it would take to get there.'

Notice also that in indirect speech the tense (past, present, or future) of the action can change to suit the time of the reporting verb (here, *said*): in the first example, *hope* becomes *hoped* and *he's not* becomes *he wasn't*; and in the second example *will* is changed to *would*.

Tip
Direct speech gives the actual words used
Indirect speech reports what someone said in the words of another speaker

People's opinions and decisions are sometimes given in a form that is rather like direct speech but doesn't have quotation marks:

6 **Punctuating speech and quotations**

> People in the country didn't know they were born, he thought.

> Dreams about loss and death, she says, help us explore our fears about mortality.

In these sentences, 'he thought' and 'she says' are not reporting actual words used by the people concerned; rather, the words are those of the writer and 'he thought' and 'she says' are a kind of aside, not referring to something actually said at a particular moment, but put in to show that the words represent a summary of what someone else thinks.

Because it is an aside, it is separated from the rest of the sentence by a pair of commas.

For more information on asides, *see* page 27.

7 Punctuating words and phrases

For **macro** and **micro** levels, *see* page 26.

Linking and separating words

As well as helping you to organize sentences and paragraphs, punctuation serves to show the connections between individual words and phrases. This is the micro-level, like a micro-climate, that we talked about in an earlier chapter. Punctuation helps to make the meaning clearer when words come together in different relationships.

Some punctuation marks link words: for example, hyphens and apostrophes. Others separate words, especially commas.

Punctuation that links words

Here are examples of punctuation that links words:

Hyphen

The hyphen is used to form compound words, especially when these are made up of three or more individual words that have a special combined meaning:

man-of-war

jack-in-the-box

If the individual words retain their own meanings, they are often spelt without hyphens:

balance of payments

a man of God

Compounds consisting of two words are now usually unhyphenated when they are written separately, or else they are spelt as one word:

table lamp

pork pie

houseboat

But you sometimes need to use a hyphen when the position of the compound can make its role unclear, especially before another noun:

a balance-of-payments crisis
(= a crisis in a country's balance of payments: without the hyphen the reader might understand it as a 'payments crisis')

a pork-pie hat
(= a hat having the shape of a pork pie)

> **Watch out!**
> for the difference between hyphens and dashes. They may look the same in ordinary writing, but in printing and word processing they are different characters.
>
> *See* the Reference section on page 69.

> **Watch out!**
> In printing and word-processing, you use an en-rule, which is longer than a hyphen, when the link has the stronger notion of 'to' or 'between'. The main uses are in a range of numbers or with names that are sharing in something:
>
> *See pages 34–6.*
>
> *the war of 1939–45*
>
> *a joint English–French venture*

a ground-to-air missile
(= a missile fired from the ground into the air)

And notice the following:

It was a town of a thousand-odd inhabitants.
(The meaning would be very different without the hyphen!)

He had applied for a small-business loan.
(The hyphen shows that it was a loan for small businesses and not a small loan for any business.)

Apostrophe

For apostrophes in names ending in s (such as *Charles's*) and other special cases, *see* the Reference section on page 79.

You use an apostrophe to show a possessive word, i.e. one that deals with ownership or possession. The rule is to add *'s*, or just an apostrophe to a plural word ending in s:

the boy's books (one boy)

the girls' books (plural: more than one girl)

the children's shoes (plural but not ending in s)

Watch out!
Do not use an apostrophe in ordinary plurals, e.g. *apple's, video's*.

See the Reference section on page 84.

Note that when a plural word ends in a letter other than s (e.g. *children* above, and other words such as *women* and *people*) you add *'s* and not s'. You only have s' when the plural form already ends in s.

In grammar, a possessive form doesn't have to be about actual ownership in the conventional sense, but can cover all sorts of relationships:

'You have not had thirty years' experience, Mrs Grindle-Jones,' he says witheringly. 'You have had one year's experience thirty times.'

This rule is explained in more detail in the Reference section on pages 78–9.

The apostrophe plus s marks the possessive and sets up a link between *year* (or *years*) and *experience*. Note the difference between the two forms: the apostrophe before the s denotes a singular *year* and the apostrophe after the s denotes plural *years*.

Most business names that were once regarded as possessive forms now omit the apostrophe, e.g. *Lloyds Bank*. But not all: e.g. *Lloyd's of London* (the insurance underwriters). Check the correct form of each name as used by the business itself.

The apostrophe is also used to mark missing letters in so-called contractions, e.g. *didn't*, *we've*, and *o'clock*. The first two types are conversational in style and are used mainly in less formal writing, although they are becoming more and more widely acceptable in print (and are used in this book, for example).

Remember that the apostrophe marks the missing letter or letters, and should be placed where that letter would be in the full form. A common mistake is to put

✘ did'nt
✘ could'nt, etc.

The correct forms are

✔ didn't
✔ couldn't, etc.

You can find more information about this use in the Reference section on pages 82–3.

because the apostrophe replaces the missing *o* in *not*.

> ***Watch out!***
> for the difference between *its* and *it's*:
>
> *The box has a label on its* (= possessive) *side.*
>
> *It's* (= *it is*) *difficult to read the label.*

See the Reference section on page 95.

Punctuation that separates words

Here are examples of punctuation that separates words:

Commas with nouns

The comma is the key to marking off words you want to separate or keep distinct:

> The room had a table, an armchair, a built-in wardrobe, and a comfortable enough bed.

The Oxford comma

Some publishing houses use this final comma in all cases. Oxford University Press is one of them, and so the practice is often called the 'Oxford comma'.

In this sentence the commas mark off items in a kind of list. You don't have to put a comma before the *and* that marks the last item in the list (*poor housing* in the example below):

> They are hit hardest by traffic fumes, factory pollution and poor housing.

But when the grouping of nouns is more complex, when for example there are pairs of nouns that go together or there are compound nouns, it is advisable to use a comma before the final *and* to make the relations between words clear:

> We ordered bacon and eggs, sausage and chips, and ice cream to follow.

Commas with adjectives

When you have a series of adjectives (words that describe), you usually separate them with commas when they all refer to the same sort of thing, such as a physical state or someone's character:

> He was a stubborn, prickly old man.

But sometimes it is more effective to link two adjectives with *and*:

> He was a stubborn and prickly old man.

You do not normally need any kind of link when the adjectives have different types of reference; if, for example, one refers to colour and the other to size:

> The car stopped at a bright little cottage.

But notice the value of the comma in a sentence like this one:

> His first, angry urge was to smash the glass.

The comma shows that the first urge was angry, whereas the later urges were not (or not necessarily) angry. Without the comma the sentence would imply a series of angry urges of which this was the first.

Commas with names

You do not use a comma when **a noun denoting a person** is followed by the person's name:

Their **brother** John had come to stay.

President Bush will undergo minor surgery today.

But you use a pair of commas when a name or description follows as an aside:

Their brother, John, had come to stay.

The effect of the commas is to suggest 'their brother, who by the way was called John'.

The Egyptian President, Hosni Mubarak, denied that Egypt was building a chemical weapons plant.

Here, the word *President* is used as an ordinary word and not as a title. The name has the status of additional information.

You need commas when a name or designation is followed by a description:

Her father, a local policeman, had something to say about it.

For more about
brackets, see the
Reference section
beginning on
page 67.

Brackets and dashes

You can also use brackets and dashes, more informally, as you can with other asides:

Her father—a local policeman—had something to say about it.
Her father (a local policeman) had something to say about it.

For more about
dashes, see the
Reference section
beginning on
page 69.

Commas that avoid confusion

Commas are very useful in keeping words apart that might mean something different if read together. There are three types of special danger that you can watch out for:

■ words that can be adverbs or prepositions, such as *across*, *beyond*, *inside*, and *over*

Notice the difference between the two uses of *inside* in the following sentences:

Inside the house a party was going on.
Inside, the house had been completely refurbished.

In the first sentence, *inside* is a preposition governing *the house*, and there is no comma.

In the second sentence, *inside* is an adverb qualifying the whole sentence, and you need a comma. Without a comma, the reader could be led into thinking that *inside* was a preposition, as it is in the first sentence. The rest of the sentence makes it clear that this isn't the case, but by then your reader may well have stumbled.

■ adverbs, such as *only* and *usually*, that can refer to different parts of the sentence. The position of the comma can make a difference:

On that day only, new applicants can call in person.
On that day, only new applicants can call in person.

In the first version, *only* refers to the date, whereas in the second, it refers to the applicants.

■ words that make an idiom but that sometimes need their separate meanings, e.g. *sick and tired, now or never*:

He felt sick, and tired of waiting.

Without the comma, the separate meaning of 'sick' is lost, and the words will be understood as a phrase 'sick and tired'.

Say it now, or never mention it again.

Again, omission of the comma might cause temporary misunderstanding.

Special uses of punctuation   8

Like most useful tools, some punctuation marks are put to extra uses that are quite separate from their main roles of organizing words and sentences. For example, they are used in abbreviations and dates, and are an important part of Internet addresses.

Full stops in abbreviations

Abbreviations made up of initial letters (called **initialisms**) have traditionally contained full stops:

B.B.C., e.g., Ph.D.

The purpose of the full stops is to show that a group of letters is something other than a normal word. As abbreviations become more common and familiar, so it becomes more and more usual to omit the full stops:

BBC, eg, Ph D

Abbreviations that consist of the first few letters of a word (called **shortenings**) are still usually spelt with a full stop, because they are more likely to be mistaken (if only momentarily) for words in their own right:

Mon. (= Monday), co. (= company), beg. (= beginning), no. (= number)

Checklist

There are four main kinds of abbreviation:

initialisms made from first letters: *BBC, BBC, YOU*, i.e.

shortenings, usually the beginnings of words: *Mon., Tues., Lieut.*

contractions in which the middle of the word is left out: *Dr, Mrs*

acronyms, based on the first letters of words, that are words in their own right: *radar, nimby* (= not in my back yard). Strictly speaking, acronyms are not abbreviations and they never have full stops.

Single-letter shortenings usually keep the full stop:

> b. 1956 (= born in 1956)
> d. 2001 (= died in 2001)
> p. 32 (= page 32, in references; also pp. = pages)

Tip
There is a lot of variation of style in abbreviations. Decide your own style and stick to it.

Contractions (shortenings with the middle part of the word left out) tend to omit the full stop:

> Dr, Mr, Mrs, Ms, actg (= acting)

Punctuation in numbers

Various conventions are used to organize the written form of numbers:

- Commas mark off thousands in longer numbers, e.g. *1,500,000.*

- Full stops mark decimal points in fractions and financial figures, e.g. *10.5%, £24.99.*

AmE

- Full stops (or, especially in American practice, colons) separate hours and minutes in expressions of time, e.g. *9.30 a.m., 12:15 p.m.*

Punctuation in dates

AmE

In American practice it is usual to put the month first, followed by the day: *08.17.02.*

Dates usually need no punctuation when they are written in full:

> 17 August 2002

When the three parts are all written as numbers you normally need full stops or slashes between them:

> 17.8.02 or 17.08.02 or 17/8/02 or 17/08/02

Punctuation in addresses

Postal addresses

Commas are used to separate the parts of a postal address when these are written on the same line:

27 Glenorchy Terrace, Edinburgh, EH9 2DQ

Tip
Note that it is usual now to omit the comma between the house number and the street name.

But commas are often omitted from an address written on separate lines, for example on an envelope:

27 Glenorchy Terrace
Edinburgh
EH9 2DQ

Internet addresses

Full stops divide the parts of an Internet website or email address, and the whole address comes after the prefix 'http' (= hypertext transfer protocol) separated by a colon and two forward slashes:

http://www.oup.co.uk

http://www.askoxford.com

Tip
Use the **askoxford** website for answers to your queries about language

In email addresses, the person or group addressed comes first, followed by an 'at' sign @ and the domain name:

sales@oup.co.uk

The correct placing of full stops is very important in Internet addresses. To avoid possible confusion, many people omit the full stop at the end of a sentence when such an address comes at the end:

Visit our website at www.askoxford.com

Avoid putting a full stop or other punctuation at the end, as this can be mistaken for part of the address.

When to use capital letters

Always begin a new sentence with a capital letter, even if the sentence is not 'complete':

Liberty means responsibility. That is why most men dread it.

Someone watches over us when we write. Mother. Teacher. Shakespeare. God.

You should also use capital letters for other reasons:

■ in names of people and places, e.g. *Kate, Sanjay, Florence, St Kitts & Nevis, Mount Everest, the Irish Sea*;

■ for the main words in titles of books, plays, pieces of music, pictures, newspapers, etc., e.g. *Love Among the Single Classes, The Times, Flight of the Bumble Bee, Hunters in the Snow*;

■ in titles of people, e.g. *the Archbishop of Westminster, His Majesty the King*;

■ in words for particular institutions, e.g. *the Government, the State, the Crown, the Church, the Labour Party, Islam*;

■ in geographical descriptions that are recognized names, e.g. *Northern Ireland* (but *northern England*, which is purely geographical);

■ in names of special days and festivals, e.g. *the Ascension, Christmas Day, Hanukkah*.

Part B: Reference section
Contents

In Part B, we will look at punctuation from the other end. Each punctuation mark has its own heading followed by a description of its main roles. When roles overlap, you will find a reference to another heading, either in this section or in Part A.

Use this section to check the main features of each punctuation mark. At the end of this section there is a trouble-shooting checklist of common errors, which lists the main pitfalls people fall into and refers you to other parts of the book where a particular problem is dealt with in more detail.

Full stop (.)

This is also known as a *period, point, full point,* or *stop.* The term *period* dates from the 16th century and originally meant a complete or well-formed sentence; then in the 17th century it came to be applied to the punctuation mark that ended it, along with the other names mentioned. The name *full stop* (now the most familiar term in everyday use) occurs in Shakespeare (see the quotation above), where it is used as an exhortation from one speaker to another to cut short his speech.

Full stop in sentences

The main use of the full stop is to mark the end of a sentence when this is a statement. In a short sentence it is often the only punctuation mark that is needed:

Joe counted the rest of the money in the box and frowned.

A full stop can also mark 'incomplete' sentences when they lack a verb or have words that are understood, as in the opening of *Nice Work* by David Lodge (1988):

Monday, January 13th, 1986. Victor Wilcox lies awake, in the dark bedroom, waiting for his quartz alarm clock to bleep.

Or in this statement from Bill Gates of Microsoft of what business is all about:

I think business is very simple. Profit. Loss. Take the sales, subtract the costs, you get this big positive number.

So called 'elliptical' sentences of this kind are common in literature for special effect:

It was a dream breakfast. Bacon and egg and sausage and beans and tomatoes. All steaming hot. A rack of toast with marmalade and butter in dishes. And a big mug of tea.

We're here on holiday. For a rest. We can do without people crashing in through the kitchen window.

Full stop

Come, the full stop.

Shakespeare, *The Merchant of Venice*, III.1 (1596)

No iron can stab the heart with such force as a full stop put just at the right place.

Isaac Babel (Russian writer, 1894–1939)

When the sentence is a question or exclamation, you use a question mark or exclamation mark instead. Both of these marks include a full stop in their forms (see question mark, page 71 and exclamation mark, page 73).

Full stop in abbreviations

The use of full stops in abbreviations is gradually disappearing, because the original intention of showing that a group of letters is not an ordinary word but a collection of initials is no longer so important. Abbreviations are increasingly spelt without full stops when they consist entirely of capital letters (*AGM, NNE, TUC*) or a mixture of capital and small letters (*BSc, Dr, Ms*).

But full stops are still usual when the abbreviation is made up entirely of small letters, because in this form they are less immediately recognizable as abbreviations rather than words (*a.o.b., p.m., t.b.a.*).

Abbreviations consisting of the first few letters of words, often called 'shortenings', are usually spelt with a full stop at the end (*co., Oct., Tues.*).

If an abbreviation with a full stop comes at the end of a sentence, you do not need to add another full stop, unless another piece of punctuation, such as inverted commas or a bracket, come after the abbreviation: *Bring your own pens, pencils, rulers, etc.* but *Bring your own things (pens, pencils, rulers, etc.)*.

There is a special kind of abbreviation, called an *acronym*, that goes one stage further than an ordinary abbreviation and becomes a word in its own right. Acronyms are often written with small letters, can form plurals, and are pronounced as syllables rather than as the sequence of letters from which they are made. Examples include *radar* (= radio detection and ranging), *scuba* (= self-contained underwater breathing apparatus), and names of organizations such as *Nato* (= North Atlantic Treaty Organization). Because acronyms are fully-fledged words, they do not have full stops.

Full stop in other uses

Full stops are used to mark off units of money (*£24.99, $100.50*), to show decimal fractions (*17.5%*), and to separate hours and minutes in showing time (*12.30 p.m.*; but in American English a colon is used, e.g. *12:30 p.m.*).

Full stops are also used to separate the parts of an email address or website name:

```
http://www.oup.co.uk

sales@oup.co.uk
```

Comma (,)

The term *comma* dates from the 16th century and is derived from a Greek word *komma*, which literally meant 'a piece cut off', and came to be used of a phrase or group of words and then the punctuation mark associated with them.

The comma works primarily as a separator. Its main role is to indicate the structure of sentences and to make their meaning clear by showing which words belong together and which do not. It usually represents the natural breaks and pauses that you make in speech, and can mark groups of words, or phrases, as well as single words:

Maybe, as a general rule, the fewer commas a person used, the more ruthless a tyrant he would prove to be if placed in a position of power.

Nicholson Baker, *Room Temperature* (1990)

The comma separating phrases

You often need a comma to mark off parts of a sentence that are linked by words such as *and*, *but*, and *yet* (called conjunctions), and also by so-called 'subordinating' conjunctions such as *if* and *although*. This is especially important when the subject of the sentences changes or is repeated:

The interviewer hesitated, and when he asked the next question he sounded faintly embarrassed.

The use of a comma in these cases is especially important when the sentence is fairly long:

> If we moor a tiny boat at some fixed point in the pond, the boat will bob up and down rhythmically as the waves pass under it.

It is not normally correct to join the clauses of a compound sentence without a conjunction (the so-called 'comma splice'):

> ✗ His was the last house, the road ended with him.

You should either put in a conjunction such as *and*, or use a semicolon:

> His was the last house, and the road ended with him.

or

> His was the last house; the road ended with him.

It is also incorrect to separate a subject from its verb with a single comma:

> ✗ Those with the lowest incomes and no other means, should get the most support.

This should be

> Those with the lowest incomes and no other means should get the most support.

A comma also separates parts of a sentence that balance or complement each other:

> The meeting is not cancelled, only postponed.

> It was getting warmer, but not yet warm enough for their picnic.

A comma is used to introduce direct speech, especially when this is continued after a reporting verb such as *say* or *ask*:

> A former headmistress once said, 'If Constance had nothing else to read, she'd read the label on a jam jar!'

A comma can help to avoid ambiguity or momentary misunderstanding:

> Inside, the house was both smaller and larger than it looked.

> She had loved, herself, as a young girl.

When an adverb or adverbial phrase such as *already*, *moreover*, *still*, *yesterday*, *personally*, or *next day* comes at the beginning of a sentence, you need to put a comma after it when there would be a natural pause in speaking:

> Personally, I have always looked upon cricket as organized loafing.

> On the plus side, death is one of the few things that can be done as easily lying down.

> Crucially, his confessions of major fraud were ignored.

> As a townee, she'd had little experience of the countryside.

> Still, he did at least show encouraging signs of intending to leave.

The same applies to subordinate clauses that come at the beginning of a sentence. These can be based on present participles (forms ending in *-ing*) or begin with a word such as *although*, *when*, *if*, or *because*:

> Putting the plates down, Bella sat in a chair and pulled Jinny towards her.

> If Jane does not get well soon, we will call the doctor.

> When our vital interests are challenged, we will act.

A comma is especially important after the word *however* when this comes at the beginning of a sentence and means 'by contrast' or 'on the other hand':

> However, a good deal of discretion is left in the hands of area managers.

But you do not use a comma after *however* when it comes before an adjective or adverb and it means 'no matter how much':

> However large it was, it was not going to be large enough for this.

The comma used in pairs

You use commas in pairs to mark off parts of a sentence that are asides or not part of the main statement:

> The universe that we know, of course, is a tiny fragment of the actual universe.

> Despite his good intentions, however, all thought of Alice slipped from his mind.

> But memories, she knew, must be painful for him.

> She felt she had, at last in India, come to the right place.

Remember that pairs of commas do the same sort of job as brackets, and you need both commas just as you need both brackets. (On this point see page 67.)

You also use commas to separate a relative clause (one beginning with *which*, *who*, *whom*, or *whose*) when this is adding extra information and the sentence would make sense without it:

> The money, which totals more than half a million, comes from three anonymous donors.

But you do not use commas when the clause identifies a person or thing you have just mentioned and is an essential part of the meaning:

> What happened to the man who called last week?

The comma separating words

A comma is used to separate adjectives of the same type (i.e. covering the same range of meaning) that come before a noun:

> They were behaving like horrible, craven infants.

> an idyllic, unspoilt countryside

The comma can be replaced by *and* between a pair of adjectives to make a stronger effect:

> They were behaving like horrible and craven infants.

When the adjectives have a different range of reference (for example, size and colour), and could not normally be separated by the word *and*, it is usual to omit the comma:

> ✓ He was wearing his baggy brown jacket.

> ✗ He was wearing his baggy and brown jacket.

> ✓ She gave him an old Dutch painting

> ✗ She gave him an old and Dutch painting..

But you can put a comma in to give extra emphasis to each of the adjectives, and this is quite common in descriptive writing:

> They were put down in a wide, dark road.

(The effect of the comma is to make the sentence equivalent to:

> They were put down in a wide road that was also very dark.)

But note that you always leave the comma out when the last adjective has a strong connection with the noun, so that the two words effectively make a set term or phrase (in the examples, *foreign correspondent*, *old lady*, and *grey seal*):

> the newspaper's new foreign correspondent

> a little old lady

> a beautiful grey seal

Commas are used to separate items in a list or sequence. You do not need a comma before *and* in the last item, although some people put one and this is not incorrect:

> It is as though we were to speak of dogs, lions, weasels, bears, hyenas, pandas, and otters all in one breath.

An alternative is to include a comma in this position only when it is needed to add clarity:

> For breakfast they had tea, toast and marmalade, and eggs.

(The final comma clarifies the special link between *toast* and *marmalade*, which is effectively a phrase in its own right.)

Omit the comma between nouns that occur together in the same grammatical role in a sentence (called apposition), when the second identifies the first. Very often it is a name:

> Her friend Helen had also been playing on the beach.

> Their dog Gruff would be waiting at the gate.

But you need a pair of commas when the second noun is treated as a piece of extra information and is not part of the main structure of the sentence:

> They could see the holiday house, Rose Cottage, in the distance.

Semicolon (;)

The term dates from the 17th century and, as its name suggests, literally means 'half a colon', although this literal meaning is a little deceptive in regard to its modern function.

The main role of the semicolon is to mark a division that is stronger than a comma but less strong than a full stop.

The two parts of a sentence divided by a semicolon should balance each other, rather than lead from one to the other (in which case you probably need a colon):

> To err is human; to blame it on the other party is politics.

> The rich don't have children; they have heirs.

> Charlotte had gone on to university; Luke was now at sixth-form college.

You will find the semicolon especially useful to make a stronger division in a sentence that already contains commas:

> He'd rather that I'd stayed at home, and then he would continue to make jokes about me being the last housewife in captivity; or else that I had found some trendy, highly-paid job in the media.

> There was more fresh meat and vegetables, and an improvement in the food supply, so that not so many people died of starvation or diseases caused by malnutrition; transport improved, so that food shortages in a particular area could be remedied.

You could write the last piece as two separate sentences, but the balance between the two statements would not be so clear.

At a comma, stop a little. At a semicolon, somewhat more.

Richard Hodges (1644)

Colon (:)

The ancient reformers of language invented three manner of pauses ... The second they called colon.

George Puttenham (1589)

The term dates from the 16th century and is derived from a Greek word *kolon* meaning 'a limb' and in grammar 'a clause'; like other names it later came to denote the associated punctuation mark. (It is a different word from the one referring to the intestines.)

While a semicolon links two balanced statements, a colon leads from the first statement to the second. Typically it links a general or introductory statement to an example, a cause to an effect, or a premise to a conclusion. (In many cases a conjunction such as *so* or *for example* could be introduced between the two halves.)

> When we parted he offered me a choice: maintenance for myself and the children, or the house and all its contents outright, and nothing else.

> Dear old Grandpa: he'd only been here twenty minutes and he was bored already.

> I feel angry: do I look angry?

But the difference between semicolon and colon is not always clear-cut. In a sentence like the one below you could easily replace the colon with a semicolon to give a stronger sense of balance between the two statements:

> That is not what a scrupulous, principled government does: that is what a weak, cynical, vacillating government does.

You also use a colon to introduce a list of items. You can interpret the idea of a 'list' quite broadly; it doesn't have to be a list of physical things in the conventional sense but can, for example, consist of descriptive words as in the second example below:

> The very wealthy employed a variety of servants: cooks, butlers, footmen, grooms, chambermaids, housemaids, laundry maids, and scullery maids.

> The best thing a pilot can be is careful: sober, meticulous, receptive, and careful.

In some older printing, you sometimes see a dash after the colon when a formal list of items is displayed beneath on separate lines. This is unnecessary but not wrong.

You can use a colon to give more emphasis or drama to a statement in direct speech:

She suddenly burst out: 'Guy's very unhappy. What can we do for him?'

In American English, a colon is sometimes used instead of a comma after the initial greeting in a letter:

Dear Dr Harvey:

Brackets () []

The term dates in this meaning from the 18th century, and is a development of the term used in building, which dates from the 16th century. The form comes from a Latin word *bracae* meaning 'breeches', which the Romans are thought to have acquired from their neighbours in Gaul.

The brackets you will use most often in writing are round brackets or parentheses () and square brackets [].

You use round brackets:

■ to add an explanation or extra comment:

Each age finds its own killer (in our day, for example, the cigarette and the motor car).

This can sometimes be a complete sentence:

Personal cleanliness was improved by an increase in the production of soap and of cotton clothing (the latter could be washed more easily and more frequently than woollen garments).

■ to show words that are optional or reflect doubt in the writer's mind:

> The dust has yet to settle on this contentious issue but a consensus (perhaps incorrect) seems to be emerging.

■ to give references and statistical information, such as a person's dates or the source of a quotation:

> William Hogarth (1697–1764) satirized the scandal in his famous caricature Gin Lane.

> To be or not to be, that is the question (Shakespeare, Hamlet)

Note that punctuation coming at the end of the part in brackets goes outside the brackets when it belongs to the sentence as a whole, and inside them when it belongs to the words inside, especially when these form a separate sentence beginning with a capital letter:

> Jean Baptiste Lamarck (1744–1829), the great French biologist and early evolutionist.

> In 1742–3 the output of British spirits was 8 million gallons (including 7 million gallons of gin).

> He grinned. (He'd had a lot more to drink than she had.)

There is another kind of brackets, square brackets, but you won't need to use these much except in more formal writing and editing. They are mainly used to put in extra information to clarify a point that might otherwise be unclear or ambiguous to the reader:

> Kate had said that after Joanna had been to see her, she felt much better about it all.

Is it Kate or Joanna that felt much better? It could be either, and so the reporting sentence needs an addition such as:

> Kate had said that after Joanna had been to see her, she [Kate] felt much better about it all.

Dash (—)

The reason for the name, which dates from the 16th century, is uncertain. It may be connected with the idea of a 'dash' or 'stroke' of the pen, but this meaning of the word *dash* is not recorded until a later date.

In formal printing there are two types of dash, although not many people are aware of the difference. There is a so-called en-rule (-) and a longer em-rule (—). The em-rule is the one used as a dash in general use, while the shorter en-rule is used for some special purposes (e.g. to mark a range of dates or numbers, as in *1801–2* and *pages 51–9,* and to link words when the notion is 'between', as in *American–Chinese hostility*).

Note that, in printing, both these dashes are longer than a hyphen.

It is worth knowing the difference if you do a lot of word-processing, because most programs are able to distinguish them (although you may have to use a special combination of keystrokes).

But there is no real distinction in ordinary writing, where the dash is done freehand and varies considerably in length. You use this either singly or in pairs for several purposes:

- A single dash can introduce words that explain or elaborate on what has gone before:

  Each school can, once again, become what it was always meant to be—a building that has four walls with tomorrow inside.

  You can also use a colon here, but the dash is more relaxed and conversational in style.

  But individuals do not evolve—they can only grow, reproduce, and die.

  Here you could use a semicolon instead, but the effect would again be more formal.

*In modern wit
all printed trash
is Set off with
num'rous breaks
– – and dashes
—.*

Jonathan Swift (1733)

■ A single dash can also introduce an extra point or after-thought:

> She had always imagined he would go on for years—and perhaps he would.

> Familiarity breeds contempt—and children.

■ You use a single dash when you want to break off a statement without completing it. This is normally only done in giving direct speech, especially in fiction:

> 'It's just I think it would have been a bit nicer if—'

(A full stop at the end of a sentence ending like this is optional.)

■ You can use a pair of dashes to mark asides and added comments that do not form part of the main statement. Dashes form a more distinct break than commas would and usually have a more casual or conversational feel:

> It sounded—yes, that was it—like something heavy being dragged across the stony yard in front of the cottage.

> Then too—after an involuntary cry of shock—he had lowered his eyes as if afraid of embarrassing me.

Slash (/)

The more formal printing name for this is *oblique* (from Latin *obliquus*, meaning 'sloping') or *solidus* (a Latin word for a coin corresponding to our shilling), and it is sometimes also called *stroke*.

The slash has a number of special uses at word level:

■ to mark alternatives to *or* in certain contexts:

> Dear Sir/Madam

> name of parent/guardian

> he/she

- in some abbreviations:

  a / c (= account)

  c / o (= care of)

  km / h (= kilometres per hour, as an alternative to *kph*)

- instead of a dash to show a range of places or dates:

  the financial year 2001/2

  the London/Paris flight

At phrase and sentence level, the slash is conventionally used to show the ends of lines in poetry when this is written in continuous form:

  Tyger Tyger, burning bright / In the forests of the night

The slash (here called a forward slash) is also used to mark off the parts of an Internet domain name or website (and a double slash is used after the colon of the initial prefix http):

  http://www.bbc.co.uk/radio4/news

A reverse slash (called a *backslash*) is used more generally in computing to mark off different levels in the path name of a file, beginning with the name of the drive and ending with the file name:

  C:\my documents\personal\invitation.doc

Question mark (?)

Main uses

You normally use a question mark to show that what you have said is a question:

  Are they arriving tomorrow?

  Where shall I put the chair?

  Is that you?

  Who will cure the nation's ill?

It is sometimes used when the question is put in the form of a statement, to reflect a rising intonation in speech:

> She told you that?
>
> Surely they are the same?
>
> I wonder if I might interrupt you?

You do not use a question mark when the question is expressed in indirect speech, i.e. it is reported rather than expressed in the original words used:

> He asked what time it was.

But you do use a question mark in so-called 'tag questions' such as *did she?* and *aren't you?*, which are really emphatic statements put in the form of questions:

> She didn't agree, did she?
>
> You're much better now, aren't you?

Double question marks

Using more than one question mark (??, ???, and so on) to express a strong feeling or doubt in a question that doesn't expect an answer (a so-called rhetorical question) is acceptable in informal writing but should not be used in reports, business letters, and other more formal contexts:

> What sort of people are they??

A single question mark in round brackets is a standard convention used to express a doubt about something, such as a date:

> Julius Caesar was born in (?) 100 BC and murdered in 44 BC.

Exclamation mark (!)

You use an exclamation mark to show in writing something that is normally said loudly or strongly in speech. There are several reasons you might do this:

■ to attract attention;

■ to tell someone what to do;

■ to express surprise;

■ because you think something is interesting or exciting.

The most common uses are to express in writing words that do the following in speech:

■ call someone or attract their attention:

John! Where are you?

■ give a command or warning:

Do as I say!

Watch out!

But don't use an exclamation mark in an instruction that is expressed as a statement with a verb such as *advise*, *urge*, and *recommend*

We urge you to take immediate action.

I recommend that you write a letter of complaint.

■ indicate a strong feeling of absurdity, surprise, approval, dislike, regret, etc., especially after *how* or *what*:

How extraordinary!

What an appalling suggestion!

Aren't they strange!

And then he kissed her!

Why, Andy, you've been hurt!

■ express a wish or a feeling of regret:

> I'd love to see the children!

> If only you had said!

■ in speech, indicate someone calling out or shouting:

> 'Bert!' he shouted, and jumped down the stairs three at a time.

The exclamation mark also occurs in literature, especially in poetry, to express a strong feeling or idea that the poet wants to share with the reader (or hearer):

> O, weep for Adonais! (Shelley)

> All too soon the tiny breakfast, Trolley-bus and windy street! (Betjeman)

You do not normally need to use the exclamation mark in this way in normal writing, but you can use it in informal writing to add emphasis to an interesting or noteworthy point you are making (the equivalent of *would you believe it?* or *yes he really did*, etc.). It is usual to put the exclamation mark in round brackets immediately after the word or phrase that you are highlighting:

> There are ten (!) children in the family now.

This, and the use of double exclamation marks or a combination of exclamation mark and question mark, should only be used in personal letters and other informal types of writing such as emails:

> My goodness, I was angry!!!

> Are you being serious?!

It is very important, as a matter of good style, not to be tempted to use exclamation marks just to add an artificial sense of drama or excitement to a piece of writing that is essentially routine or straightforward.

Quotation marks (' ' " ")

These are also called *inverted commas*. Their chief role is to indicate speech and quotations, in which words used by someone else are quoted in their original form. In writing it is common to use double quotation marks (" "), although in printing practice varies between the double and single style (' ').

Single quotation marks are more usual in British printing and double marks in American printing, but the distinction is not always so clear-cut in general usage.

AmE

The rules given here are based on British practice, and any differences in American English are noted.

It is important to know the difference between direct speech and indirect speech:

Direct speech gives the words as spoken:

'Don't call me soft,' he said, and kicked her on the ankle.

Indirect speech turns the words used into a 'reported' form so that they come from the writer and not the person who originally used them:

He told her not to call him soft, and kicked her on the ankle.

You use quotation marks in direct speech, but not in indirect speech.

In direct speech, the quoted words form the main structure of the sentence, built round a verb such as *say* or *ask*. The closing quotation mark normally comes after a final full stop, or after any other punctuation that forms part of the quotation, such as an exclamation mark or question mark:

He went back to the kitchen, saying: 'I've done some soup and a salad.'

'Well?' he said at last. 'Isn't it for me?'

When the quoted speech is followed or interrupted by a reporting verb such as *say*, *shout*, etc., the punctuation that divides the sentence is put inside the quotation marks:

> 'If people can be taught evil,' she beams, 'they can be taught kindness too.'

When your writing includes several speakers having a conversation or exchange, the words start on a new line when there is a change of speaker:

> Harriet said: 'When do you suppose Callard heard?'
>
> 'Yesterday, I should think.'
>
> 'Then he may still contact you.'
>
> 'Oh yes, I'm not worrying.'
>
> 'If he doesn't, what will you do?'
>
> 'I don't know. I haven't thought.'

Notice that the identities of the speakers are not normally repeated each time. The reader has to keep track of the alternating speakers and may need to refer back to the beginning of the conversation. This is an accepted convention, but if the exchange continues for a long time it is a good idea to help readers by reminding them occasionally of which speaker is which. If there are more than two speakers, you need to do this more often.

The rules are slightly different when you include words as a quotation within a sentence and these do not form the main part of the sentence.

There are several reasons you might want to do this:

- to quote a word or phrase from someone else, or one that you have already used and want to discuss further:

  > These 'captains of industry' often risked their entire fortunes.

■ to indicate a word that has a special status, or is one that your readers might not recognize (either at all or in the meaning you are using). In this type, the writer will often go on to explain the term (and in the following example certainly should):

> The aptest name for my approach to understanding how things work is probably 'hierarchical reductionism'.

If a quoted word or phrase comes at the end of a sentence or coincides with a comma, the punctuation that belongs to the sentence as a whole is placed outside the quotation marks, because the quotation is not part of the main structure:

> It is technically incorrect to talk about bat 'radar', since they do not use radio waves.

> It can hardly be a coincidence that no language on earth has ever produced the expression 'as pretty as an airport'.

In American English, however, it is usual to place quotation marks outside the sentence punctuation (and note the more characteristic double quotation marks):

AmE

> Thomas Henry Huxley once defined science as "organized common sense."

When a quotation occurs within a quotation, the inner quotation is put in double quotation marks if the main quotation is in single marks (or vice versa, especially in American practice):

British 'What do you mean, "news"?'

American "What do you mean, 'news'?"

In the following example, the writer is quoting what a person (called Phipps) said, and Phipps himself is quoting what someone else said:

> 'He said,' said Phipps gleefully, '"Yes, they have more money."'

This is a fairly unusual alignment that tends to occur mainly in fiction. In ordinary writing it is best avoided whenever possible, as it can be quite confusing to the reader.

Apostrophe (')

The term is recorded from the early 17th century and comes from a Greek word *apostrophos* meaning 'turning away' and hence 'omission' or 'elision', which is the meaning relevant here. Like other names for punctuation marks, *apostrophe* originally referred to the process involved and only later to the mark used for it. It was commonly used in Greek and Latin to mark dropped letters in manuscripts (for example, *tertius* meaning 'third' was written as *t'cius*), and this is the use of the apostrophe that was first adopted in English in the 16th century, especially by the early printers.

The use of the apostrophe to show a possessive form (as in *the man's head*) is much later, however. It occurs only rarely in the First Folio (1623) of Shakespeare in this role, and it appears in modern editions of his plays because editors have changed the convention. Some people claim that the possessive form *'s* is historically a contraction of *his* (e.g. *Henry his name* = *Henry's name*) but this is not correct: it is derived from an Old English inflection that involved the adding of a final *-s* to mark a possessive form.

The rules for using apostrophes as possessive markers have always been unstable (and continue to be), and the main conventions were established as late as the 19th century. Indeed, some grammarians of that time questioned the possessive use because it did not involve an omission of letters; so this was still regarded even then as its primary function.

Apostrophes in possessive words

Despite its shaky history, the main role of the apostrophe in modern English is still to show possession or association, as in *Penny's house* and *the bank's address*.

If the noun is singular (i.e. it denotes one person or thing) you form the possessive by adding *'s*:

the cat's paws (one cat)

the bus's windows (one bus)

Mary's hair

If the noun is plural (i.e. it denotes more than one person or thing) and ends in -s you add an apostrophe after the s:

the cats' paws **(several cats)**

the Smiths' house **(a family of people called Smith)**

If the noun is plural and ends in a letter other than -s, the possessive is formed by adding 's:

the children's clothes

the people's cars

the sheep's hoofs

(In the last case, there is no way of knowing whether there are several sheep or only one, and so it is often better to rephrase this type of possessive to make it clear what you mean.)

The apostrophe is rapidly disappearing in company names and other commercial uses, e.g. *Lloyds Bank, Citizens Advice Bureau*. In each case you should follow the practice of the organization itself regarding its name.

Adding another -s to names that already end in -s (such as *James*) can make an awkward sound, and this often leaves people unsure about what to do.

There is a simple rule you can follow:

■ When you would pronounce the name with an extra -s in speech, then add an 's:

James's, Dickens's, Thomas's, The Times's

■ When you would normally pronounce the name without the extra -s, then just add an apostrophe without the extra s:

Bridges', Connors', Mars', Herodotus', Xerxes'

■ With French names ending in (silent) -s or -x, add 's:

Dumas's, le Roux's

The modified word is then pronounced with a final -z.

Beware of confusing *who's* (= *who is* or *who has*) and *whose* (= *of whom*):

  ✔ Who's (= who is) there?

  ✔ Who's (= who has) done this?

  ✘ Who's (≠ who is or who has) turn is it?

  ✔ Whose turn is it?

An apostrophe should not be used in the pronouns *hers*, *its*, *ours*, *yours*, and *theirs*:

  ✘ a friend of our's

  ✔ a friend of ours

  ✘ the house is their's

  ✔ the house is theirs

A common mistake is to confuse *its*, which is a possessive word, and *it's*, which is a contraction if 'it is' or 'it has':

  ✘ The dog was licking it's paw.

  ✔ The dog was licking its paw.

  ✔ It's (= it is) time to go.

  ✔ It's (= it has) been raining.

Apostrophes in contractions

You need an apostrophe to mark letters that have been omitted in forms known as 'contractions' (e.g. *they've*, *wouldn't*). There are not many of these left in modern English. Although they are found increasingly in print (in this book, for example), they are still widely associated with the informality of speech, and some more traditionally-minded people frown on them in more formal contexts. For this reason it is advisable to use the full forms in documents in which it is important to make a good impression, such as CVs and job applications, unless you know what your readers' attitude to contracted forms is likely to be (e.g. some companies have a more informal writing style as a matter of course).

The most common contractions are based on a pronoun and verb:

Full form	Contraction
I am	I'm
I had	I'd
I have	I've
I will or shall	I'll
I would	I'd
you are	you're
you had	you'd
you have	you've
you will or shall	you'll
you would	you'd
he is	he's
he had	he'd
he has	he's
he will or shall	he'll
he would	he'd
it is	it's (but beware of confusion with the possessive *its*: see page 95)
it had	it'd (awkward and best avoided)
it has	it's
it will or shall	it'll (awkward and best avoided)
it would	it'd (awkward and best avoided)
she is	she's
she had	she'd

she has	she's
she will or shall	she'll
she would	she'd
they are	they're
they had	they'd
they have	they've
they will or shall	they'll
they would	they'd

Note that the contractions based on *have* are only used when *have* is an auxiliary verb, i.e. it is used with another verb to form a special tense:

✔ He's bought a new car.

✘ He's a new car.

✔ They've got a cheek.

✘ They've a cheek.

In more casual English, this rule is applied flexibly when the contracted word is *have*, and it is possible to say, for example:

✔ I've a new car.

✔ We've several of those.

There is another group based on a verb + *not*. The verb is always one that can be followed by *not*, i.e. an auxiliary or 'modal' verb like *be*, *can*, *do*, *have*, or *ought*, or one of the verbs *dare* and *need* which behave in a special way:

Full form	Contraction
are not	aren't
can not	can't
could not	couldn't

dare not	daren't
did not	didn't
do not	don't
does not	doesn't
had not	hadn't
has not	hasn't
have not	haven't
is not	isn't
may not	mayn't
might not	mightn't (very informal)
need not	needn't
ought not	oughtn't
should not	shouldn't
will not	won't
would not	wouldn't

Notice that the apostrophe comes between the *n* and the *t* because it stands for the missing letter *o*:

✗ does'nt

✔ doesn't

Some words used in poetry and literature are shortened or contracted with an apostrophe, e.g. *e'er* (= ever), *tho'* (= though), *o'er* (= over). These words are not normally used in ordinary writing.

Words that are shortened by omission of letters from the beginning of longer words do not need an apostrophe when they are established in their own right, e.g. *cello* (= violoncello), *flu* (= influenza), *plane* (aeroplane).

An apostrophe is also used in some Irish names beginning with *O*, e.g. *O'Connor*, *O'Donnell*. Note that the letter following the apostrophe should be a capital letter.

| ## Apostrophes in plural forms

An apostrophe is used to show a plural in a limited range of words:

■ short words ending in a vowel, especially *o*, that might not be recognized otherwise:

do   do's
(because *dos* looks odd and *does* would be confusing)

■ pronouns used as nouns:

The cats were all she's
(because *she* is not primarily a noun and *shes* would be unfamiliar)

Beware of using an apostrophe in a word that is neither a possessive nor a special case but an ordinary plural. You sometimes see this on shop signs, and so it is sometimes known as the 'grocer's apostrophe'. Words ending in *-o* are especially vulnerable to this error (probably because of confusion with the *do's* type), but you also find it in quite harmless words such as *apples* and *pears*:

✗ video's for hire

✗ apple's 30p a pound

Avoid this at all costs: it is one of the key stigmas that will mark you as illiterate.

Apostrophes in abbreviations

It is no longer necessary to use an apostrophe to form the plurals of abbreviations and single letters, except when clarity calls for it:

Several MPs were standing around.

Dot your i's and cross your t's

An apostrophe is needed to make a possessive form of an abbreviation:

> The BBC's decision to go ahead with the broadcast was widely criticized.

Hyphen (-)

The word and the device both date from the 16th century. The name is derived from a Greek word *huphen* meaning 'together'. The ancient Greeks also used a linking hyphen, except that it was a curved sign under words rather than a straight line put between them.

The hyphen was used much more widely in the past to indicate words that were formed from other words (e.g. in compound forms such as *to-day* and *with-out*). In modern English its use is much more restricted, and the so-called 'spelling' hyphen, in which the hyphen is a regular feature of a particular spelling, is fast disappearing. This development is very welcome, because it means that the hyphen can enjoy a more effective and useful role on those occasions when it really is indispensable.

Strictly speaking, a hyphen is shorter than a dash (in printing, about half the length), but in writing there is often little noticeable difference. Usually, however, there is no space on either side of a hyphen as there is with a dash.

The dash and the hyphen have very different roles. While the dash has an essentially separating role at sentence level, the hyphen has a linking role at word and phrase level. There is a lot of variation in general usage, and dictionaries show different practices from case to case. This can be confusing, but the following guidelines will help you to use hyphens in ways that are useful and consistent.

The hyphen has three broad roles:

- as part of a word's spelling (the spelling hyphen);

- as a means of linking words that belong together in a sentence (the syntactic hyphen);

■ to mark the division of a word that has to be split at the end of a line of print.

The last of these is largely confined to printing practice, and we can ignore it here. Most word-processing programs cater for lines of different length, making it unnecessary to divide words in this way at all. If you are interested in the subject, you can look out a dictionary that deals with this aspect, such as the *Oxford Spelling Dictionary*.

The **spelling hyphen** is used to form compound words (i.e. words made from other words put together, such as *house-plant* and *table-lamp*). But in this role it is much less common than it used to be, and tends to be used only when there is some special need, for example when the compound is a long one or when letters come awkwardly together, e.g. *free-for-all*, *multi-ethnic*, and *right-handed*.

Straightforward noun compounds are much more often spelt either as two words (*boiling point*, *credit card*, *focus group*, *garden party*) or as one. This is true when several consonants come together, which used to be a reason for putting in a hyphen (*database*, *earring*, *breaststroke*, *radioisotope*).

But you often need a hyphen when the words making the compound have a grammatical relationship with one another, e.g. *dive-bomb* (based on 'to bomb by making a dive'), *house-warming* (based on 'warming the house'), *punch-drunk* (based on 'drunk from a punch').

There are two cases in which a compound spelt as two words is made into a hyphened form or a one-word form:

■ when a verb phrase such as *take off* and *climb down* is made into nouns (*take-off*, *climbdown*);

■ when a noun compound is made into a verb (e.g. *a date stamp* but *to date-stamp*).

A spelling hyphen is also used:

■ to join a prefix ending in a vowel (such as *co-* and *neo-*) to another word (e.g. *co-opt*, *neo-realism*), although one-word forms are becoming more usual (*cooperate*, *neoclassical*);

- to separate a prefix from the main word in order to avoid confusion, e.g. to distinguish *re-cover* (= provide with a new cover) from *recover* and *re-sign* (= sign again) from *resign*;

- to join a prefix to a name or designation, e.g. *anti-American*, *ex-president*;

- to stand for a common second element in all but the last word of a list, e.g. *two-, three-, or fourfold*.

A **syntactic hyphen** is used to clarify meanings in groups of words when the associations are not clear or when there are several possible associations:

Few people these days can afford to buy hard-covered novels.

The meeting was attended by fifty-odd people.

The effect of these changes was to reduce disease-carrying pests.

They seem to have a couldn't-care-less attitude.

You should also use a hyphen to clarify the meaning of a compound that is normally spelt as separate words, when it is used before another noun:

Some journals are published quarterly, with the object of providing up-to-date findings.

Notice that when the compound comes after the verb, and not before the noun, you can spell it as separate words:

Some journals are published quarterly, with the object of providing findings that are up to date.

You do not need a hyphen in a combination of adverb ending in *-ly* and adjective qualified by it, even when it comes before the noun: *a highly competitive market*, *abundant recently published material*.

But when the adverb does not end in *-ly*, you normally need a hyphen in order to make the meaning clear: *a well-known woman*, *an ill-judged remark*.

Omission marks (...)

Omission marks (also called *ellipsis*) are a series of dots (usually three) to show that something has been left out. There are two main uses:

■ to show that a word or words have been omitted from a quotation so as to make it shorter or more convenient:

> Others ... comforted themselves with the homely proverb, that, being hanged at all, they might as well be hanged for a sheep as a lamb.

In the original version (Dickens, *Barnaby Rudge*, chapter 53), the quotation began

> Others had been desperate from the beginning, and comforted themselves [etc.].

■ to mark an interruption at the end of a sentence, either to show that a speaker did not finish it or to leave the conclusion to the reader's imagination. This use is most common in stories and narratives:

> 'If I don't pee I'll ...'

You can also use a dash for this type of omission:

> There's so many folk it's more like a party. With lots of beer and home-made bread and cheese and ham and some of my mother's special cakes and—

■ Notice that an omission that comes at the end of a sentence still has three full stops, not four, and you don't add a full stop if you have used a dash. This is because the sentence has not been finished; but the next sentence (if there is one) begins with a capital letter in the normal way.

Capital letters

Capital letters are used to spell proper names, i.e. names of people and places, e.g. *London, Concorde, the English Channel*

Some words have capital initial letters even though they are not proper names. The rules for these are given on page 54.

Avoiding common punctuation errors

The following are punctuation errors that people often make. The list cannot be exhaustive, and it is a good idea to add your own recurring problems so that you have a personalized checklist.

There are references to other parts of the book for further information in some cases.

Using too many commas

Do not use commas when you don't need to. As a general rule they mark the pauses you would make in speech, and if there is no pause there is often no need for a comma. Too many commas in a piece of writing make it disjointed and distract the reader. If you find yourself using a lot of commas it may mean you need to rephrase your sentence:

By last night, the Defense Secretary, William Perry, said, there would be over 200 tactical aircraft in the area.

This sentence contains one aside ('William Perry') within another ('the Defense Secretary ... said'). Rather than juggle these commas, it would be better to reorder the sentence:

By last night there would be over 200 tactical aircraft in the area, Defense Secretary William Perry said.

One comma instead of four!

Separating two main clauses with a comma (the 'comma splice')

Main clauses coming together in the same sentence should not be separated by a comma:

✗ God has us here only on loan, we are transitory in this vale of tears.

If you want to keep the comma, you need a linking word such as *and*. Otherwise, use a semicolon if the two parts balance or a colon if the second part leads on from the first (see pages 34–7).

✔ God has us here only on loan, and we are transitory in this vale of tears.

or

✔ God has us here only on loan; we are transitory in this vale of tears.

Alternatively, split the sentence into two:

✔ God has us here only on loan. We are transitory in this vale of tears.

Putting a comma between subject and verb

It's often tempting to put a comma between the subject and verb of a sentence when the first part is longer than usual. This is incorrect:

✗ Those with the smallest incomes and no other means, should get most support.

✔ Those with the smallest incomes and no other means should get most support.

Tip

If your punctuation seems awkward it's often a sign that you should rephrase.
Here you could say:

✔ Most support should go to those with the smallest
   incomes and no other means.

In fact this way of casting the sentence makes the essential
point, about where the support should go, much better.

Here is another example:

✘ Complete and utter oblivion, is the usual fate of a crackpot.

✔ Complete and utter oblivion is the usual fate of a crackpot.

Again there is the option of rephrasing the sentence:

✔ The usual fate of the crackpot is complete and utter
   oblivion.

Putting a comma before a *that* clause

When a clause introduced by *that* comes after a verb such as
say, *know*, *insist*, or *argue*, you should not put a comma before
that (which is a conjunction in this role):

✘ Many observers have argued, that some form of planning
   is essential.

✔ Many observers have argued that some form of planning
   is essential.

But you can have a pair of commas if an aside comes before the
that clause:

✔ The report stated, for example, that science should be
   taught to all pupils in some form or other.

Omitting one comma from a pair of separating commas

This is a very common error, especially in longer sentences that have other commas. Remember that a pair of commas mark off something that is not part of the main statement in a sentence, and so you need both, just as you need both round brackets or both dashes to separate words from their surroundings.

✗ The year is bound to involve lots of changes, all of which, I believe will be positive for everyone. (comma omitted after *believe*, probably because the writer was nervous of having three commas close together; but they are needed)

✔ The year is bound to involve lots of changes, all of which, I believe, will be positive for everyone.

✗ English life, while very pleasant is rather bland.

✔ English life, while very pleasant, is rather bland.

✗ He has chosen, instead to face one of two possible scenarios.

✗ He has chosen instead, to face one of two possible scenarios.

✔ He has chosen, instead, to face one of two possible scenarios. (two commas)

or

✔ He has chosen instead to face one of two possible scenarios. (no commas)

or

✔ Instead, he has chosen to face one of two possible scenarios. (*instead* at the beginning, followed by a comma)

Putting quotation marks in the wrong place in relation to other punctuation

Remember that sentence punctuation comes inside quotation marks in direct speech:

'Dad?' she said. 'Did you say there aren't any other houses?'

But when the quotation is not a full sentence of speech but a short phrase or group of words contained within the structure of the sentence, the quotation marks go inside the sentence punctuation:

> Only in Britain could it be thought a defect to be 'too clever by half'.

Using quotation marks in indirect speech

You only use quotation marks when you are giving the exact words someone else has said or written. If you are using indirect speech, i.e. the type that can be introduced by a word like *that*, *if*, or *whether* after the reporting verb, you should not use quotation marks:

- ✔ 'Max, can I borrow your leather jacket for a couple of weeks?' asks Cordy.

- ✘ Cordy asks Max if 'he can borrow his leather jacket for a couple of weeks.'

- ✔ Cordy asks Max if he can borrow his leather jacket for a couple of weeks.

Using too many dashes

Dashes are informal in tone and produce a loose sentence structure. In everyday writing this is often more natural and acceptable, but the effect can be too casual for more formal writing.

It is often better to use pairs of commas instead of pairs of dashes, and semicolons or colons instead of single dashes.

Confusing singular and plural forms in possessives ('s and s')

Remember that a word ending in a letter other than -s forms a possessive by adding 's, whether it is singular or plural:

> the city's cathedral
>
> women's rights
>
> the oncoming car's headlights (one car)

You add an apostrophe without an -s when a plural noun already ends in -s:

> the bosses' offices
>
> the oncoming cars' headlights

Using an apostrophe in plural nouns (the 'grocer's apostrophe')

An apostrophe should not be used to form an ordinary plural:

> ✗ a pound of tomato's
>
> ✗ a pair of handle's

Using an apostrophe in yours, hers, theirs, etc.

You do not use an apostrophe in these cases:

> ✗ a friend of our's
>
> ✔ a friend of ours

Confusing *it's* and *its*

Use *it's* (with an apostrophe) to mean 'it is' or 'it has':

It's raining.

It's been raining.

Use *its* (without an apostrophe) as a possessive word (meaning 'belonging to it'):

The cat was licking its paws.

Omitting hyphens that are needed to clarify the meaning

Hyphens are used much less than they used to be in ordinary spelling. But sometimes a hyphen is needed to make the meaning clear and avoid another possible meaning:

He would be in charge of a group of French-speaking tourists.

When I was a small-boat owner, I saw the little creature on several occasions.

It is important to re-view the films every so often.

For more examples, see page 87.

Further reading

Titles marked * are available as paperbacks

Dictionaries and style guides

A standard household dictionary gives you guidance on aspects of punctuation that affect the spelling of words, especially hyphenation and capitalization, and includes many abbreviations in common use. The following are published by Oxford; similar dictionaries are published by Chambers Harrap, HarperCollins, Penguin Books, and others. Choose one that suits you best, and bear in mind that you may need more than one for different purposes.

The Concise Oxford Dictionary (revised tenth edition, Oxford, 2001)

The Oxford Compact English Dictionary (second edition, Oxford, 2000): a shortened version of the *Concise*, which some readers may find easier to use for quick reference

*The Oxford Spelling Dictionary** (second edition, Oxford, 1995): a listing of words and their inflections, with guidance on hyphenation and word division in printing

The Oxford Guide to Style (Oxford, 2002): includes guidance on punctuation and hyphenation

*Pocket Fowler's Modern English Usage** (Oxford, 2002): an updated and shortened version of the famous book written by H. W. Fowler, with many articles on punctuation and related matters, edited by the present writer

Books on punctuation and related matters

G. V. Carey, *Mind the Stop** (London, 1939): an old book that is still useful

Eric Partridge, *You Have A Point There: A Guide to Punctuation and Its Allies** (London, 1953, reprinted many times): a longer and more detailed study that is informative and entertaining, though at times idiosyncratic

Robert Allen, *Spelling* (Oxford, 2002, in the same series as this book)

Reference books on language

Tom McArthur, *The Oxford Companion to the English Language* (Oxford, 1992): includes historical articles on punctuation

David Crystal, *The Cambridge Encyclopedia of the English Language** (Cambridge, 1995): has sections on the conventions of writing and printing, with historical background and illustrations

Websites

www.askoxford.com has much information on the everyday use of language, with a 'better writing' section that includes tips on common errors and guidance on related matters such as spelling and plain English. There is also a facility for putting questions by email to the Oxford Word and Language Service (Owls).

Glossary

Technical terms are explained at the point in the text where they are used. They are listed here with definitions for general information. Explanations of the punctuation marks themselves can be found in the Reference section beginning on page 55.

abbreviation	a shortened form of a word or phrase, including initialisms (*BBC*, *TUC*, etc.), shortenings (*Apr.*, *Sat.*, etc.), contractions (*Mr*, *Jnr*, etc.), and acronyms (*Nato*, *nimby*, etc.). Acronyms are treated as words in their own right. See page 51.
acronym	See **abbreviation** above.
adjective	a word that describes another word, e.g. *blue*, *horrible*, *pleasant*
adverb	a word that qualifies a verb or adjective, e.g. *quickly, very*. A word such as *only* can be an adjective (as in *the only one*) and an adverb (as in *I only asked*).
capital letter	a large form of a letter, e.g. A,B,C, used chiefly to begin a sentence, for the first letters of proper names, and in abbreviations
clause	a group of words that contains a verb and forms part of a sentence. A main clause makes sense by itself whereas a subordinate clause is dependent on the rest of the sentence to make sense. In the sentence *She was a child when her mother died*, *she was a child* is a main clause and *when her mother died* is a subordinate clause.

complex sentence	a sentence that contains a subordinate clause, i.e. one beginning with *because*, *if*, *which*, etc. See page 30 and **subordinate clause** below.
compound sentence	a sentence with two parts joined by a linking word such as *and* or *but*. See page 29.
consonant	any of the letters *b, c, d, f, g, h, j, k, l, m, n, p, q, r, s, t, v, w, x, z*. The letter *y* is a consonant when it is sounded as in *year* and *yoke*, but is a vowel in words such as *rhythm* and *tyre*.
contraction	See **abbreviation** above.
direct speech	speech that quotes the actual words used: see **indirect speech** below and page 41.
indirect speech	speech given in a form that reports what someone has said without quoting the actual words, e.g. *She said I was right* as distinct from *'You are right,' she said*. See page 42.
inflection	a change to the ending of a word to make it fit its grammatical context, e.g. *-ed* and *-ing* in verbs or *-s* and *-es* forming plurals of nouns
initialism	See **abbreviation** above.
intonation	the changes of pitch and tone in ordinary speech, which help to clarify the meaning, e.g. indicating that a group of words is a question, and show the speaker's attitude
main clause	See **clause** above.
noun	a noun that names a person or thing, e.g. *house*, *George*, *happiness*
paragraph	a distinct piece of writing beginning on a new line (often indented, i.e. set in

	from the margin) and conveying a single idea or theme
past participle	a form of a verb used with *be* or *have*, such as *killed*, *burnt*, or *spoken*, or as a kind of adjective, as in *the burnt cakes*
phrase	a group of words that forms part of a sentence, not usually containing a verb or making complete sense by itself
possessive	a word that indicates ownership or a similar relation, e.g. a noun as in *the **boys'** room* or ***London's** river*, or a word such as *my, her, hers, their, theirs*
prefix	a number of letters added to the beginning of a word to change its meaning, e.g. *re-* in *remarry* and *un-* in *unhappy*
preposition	a word such as *in*, *on*, or *over*, which stands before a noun as in *the book **on** the table*.
pronoun	a word such as *I, he, me*, and *us* which is used instead of a noun. Possessive pronouns are words such as *mine* and *ours*.
proper noun	a noun that refers to one particular person, place, or thing and is spelt with a capital initial, e.g. *Europe, Titanic, Shakespeare*
relative clause	a clause beginning with *who, whom, whose, which*, or sometimes *that*, e.g. *There are many people **who dislike this music***. See page 32.
sentence	a group of words that make a statement or exclamation or ask a question, beginning with a capital letter and ending in a full stop
shortening	See **abbreviation** above.
simple sentence	a sentence that contains one verb and subject, e.g. *The trees are tall*

subordinate clause	a part of a sentence that contains a verb but cannot stand by itself, e.g. one beginning with *if*, *because*, or *which*. See **clause** above.
syllable	a part of a word that can be pronounced separately, e.g. *but* and *ter* in *butter*
verb	a word that describes an action or state, e.g. *become, move, remain, take*
vowel	any of the letters *a, e, i, o, u,* and sometimes *y* (as in *rhythm:* see **consonant** above)

Permissions

Extract on p. 11 from Philippa Pearce, *Tom's Midnight Garden* (1958), reprinted by permission of the publishers, Oxford University Press

Examples on p. 36 from Tim Bowler, *River Boy* (OUP, 1999)

Index

Note: **bold** page numbers indicate major references and glossary definitions; entires in *italics* indicate specific words e.g. *it's*